"*Moving to the Earth's Beat* is an original and thought provoking exploration of his eco-despair that reads like a mystery. Chopra builds a compelling case that we have a visceral connection to the natural world, highlighting the links between psychic health and the health of the environment. Drawing on both current physics and traditional Native American beliefs, Chopra provides a hopeful vision of a way forward, including persuasive ideas about how to use the power of storytelling in the struggle to save our habitat."

– Dr. Joan Goldberg, clinical psychologist

"I really enjoyed reading *Moving to the Earth's Beat*. I found it easy to relate to the content. The focus here is on eco-despair, but the issues encountered on the way into and out of it are ones everyone deals with at some level."

- Sean Murray, CEO, RealTime Performance

"I admire *Moving to the Earth's Beat* on many levels – the brave choice to write it as a personal quest, the clear and well-organized writing style, the light but never frivolous tone that leads us through the serious, even profound content."

– Deborah Melone, poet and editor

"This book took me on an introspective, intellectual, and ultimately spiritual journey that left me feeling both hopeful and empowered. Mr. Chopra's rigorous soul-searching, sharp intellect, and warm, gentle prose heightened my appreciation of the co-creation/common ground of mind and matter and the dynamic connectedness of everything. It deepened my awe of the wondrous forces of the universe and my faith in the good we do ourselves and the earth by aligning with and being supported by those forces."

– Carol Christian, writer, psychologist

MOVING TO THE EARTH'S BEAT

The Road Back from Eco-Despair

By

A.J. Chopra

Permissions Department
The Public Press
100 Gilead Brook Road
Randolph VT 05060

ThePublicPress.com info@ThePublicPress.com

book and cover design: Michael Potts
cover photograph: Richard Goerg

1 2 3 4 5 6 7 8 9 10

For all the children

To Sally,

With warm regards,

Jit Chopra,

4/7/13

Contents

Introduction 9

Part I : Looking Inside

1. Was the problem what it seemed to be? 19
2. What I learned in the querencia 33
3. Ways out of the impasse 57
4. The end of a phase 73

Part II : Finding a way forward

5. Creating a live hypothesis 77
6. Things to keep in mind 93
7. Selecting your sources 101
8. A sequence of events 109
9. The premise 127
10. Pruning the interior landscape 137
11. Speeding the shift 157
12. Reasons for hope 181
13. What I choose to believe 191
14. Postscript 209

Acknowledgments 213

References 214

Introduction

What it's about

The funk hit me suddenly. In hindsight I can see that it had been building for a while, but when it broke out into the open it came as a surprise. It was both unexpected and hard to explain. There seemed to be nothing in my situation to be depressed about. I was in good health, had people in my life I cared about and who cared about me.

I was one of four partners in a small consulting company located in Cambridge, Massachusetts. It was doing well. When I joined it there were four people in it: two partners and two staff assistants. I made it five. Now, seven years later, there were twenty-four of us in our Harvard Square office, and another dozen in our affiliates in the U.K., Holland, and Germany.

Our business was based on work we had done to identify elements of the thought process that successful inventors use in their work. We were the first in our field to make parts of that process explicit. *The Random House Dictionary* extracted a common noun from the name of our company, Synectics, and defined it as "the study of creative processes, esp. as applied to the solution of problems by a group of diverse individuals."

Clients hired us to run problem-solving sessions for project teams when they needed to do some fresh thinking. Initially we worked primarily with engineers and scientists from the Research and Development departments of companies such as Kimberly-Clark, General Foods, Exxon, and Johnson & Johnson. Then their marketing and organization development groups discovered us.

Ours was an unusual line of work. There was no short answer to the "and-what-do-you-do" question, but it was hard to conceal how pleased we were to be doing it. We existed at the wild edges of the business world, unconstrained by its conduct and dress codes. We could work in sneakers and sandals and wear our hair long. At day's end on Fridays, staff members trickled into our second floor "living room," a roughly twenty-by-thirty-foot loft space in which we could both run sessions and party.

The long wall across from the entrance had two French doors in it. Three easels were mounted on the wall space that separated them. Black leather couches formed a big "U" in front of the easels, and an oriental rug covered the space between them. On it was a table made of a solid core door sitting on four wooden cubes cut from an old beam. Several other cubes served as end tables. A dozen or so directors' chairs provided additional seating. There was a long table behind one of the couches. When sessions were held on that floor, drinks were set out on it at the end of the day for the participants. Most welcomed that opportunity to relax after a long day, often with a working lunch and a couple of short breaks. On Fridays, it was the staff's turn to relax and party.

I enjoyed my work. I had no trouble giving it sixty or seventy-hour weeks because it energized me. It was both my work and my favorite recreation. And then, suddenly it seemed, that changed. It was as if I were my usual self one Friday evening, a different person at the end of the following week.

What happened? It took me almost a year to figure out, first, what ailed me and then to develop a remedy for it. I was, it turned out, like the miners' canary, among the early victims of an emerging virus, the one that causes eco-despair. Unlike the canary I was still walking and talking, though my spirit had a hard time getting out of bed. The first symptom was a growing awareness that our way of life had put us on a high-speed train headed for a nasty ecological crash. Then came the question that felled me: was there any reason to hope that we would be able to change course in time to avoid it, or at least to slow the train enough to minimize the damage?

I feared the answer was no. The train was propelled by a hyper-consumption lifestyle that we equated with progress and success for us as both individuals and as a species. We were addicted to it. I didn't think enough people could be convinced to quit or quit aspiring to it. In developed countries, it would mean giving up too many conveniences that we considered our birthright. Like cars and air conditioning and ever-increasing supplies of electricity and running water, both cold and hot. In the developing ones it would mean letting go of the dream of attaining that lifestyle.

The impetus for the change was not going to come from our political and business leaders. It had to come from us, the consumers. Together we had a lot of economic clout — we accounted for two-thirds of the GNP in developed countries. What we needed was a consumer uprising that forced the invention of a different economic order. But I couldn't see it happening.

I couldn't see it, because I'd lost faith in our collective good sense, and in the power of our big guns, Science and Technology. If you see your kind heading for a precipice and see no way to keep them from acting like lemmings, you are left with two choices. Stop caring about them and focus on getting the most out of your life while you can. Or get depressed. Why couldn't I settle for the first option?

I talked to therapists about my problem, but that didn't help, so I worked on it on my own. I got lucky and stumbled into an explanation of it in some books that happened to be sitting on my shelves. The authors included the psychologists Abraham Maslow and Victor Frankl.

What I heard them say was that there is a part of us that transcends the boundaries of the personal ego. It identifies with its world — with other people, with other living things, with the earth. It experiences the pain of these "others" as if it were its own. It can be deeply bothered by the way things are out there. Such as injustice, or poverty, or the abuse of children or of the environment. Not a reason to get bummed out if you feel that something can and is being done, by you or by others, about the wrong you feel needs to be set right, and that the fight can be won.

But this requires you to believe that the forces on your side have what it takes to prevail against those that create the "wrong." Difficulties arise if you lose that faith. You are then left with two choices: recover that faith or live with your pain.

This book tells the story of how I regained hope that we could change our ways quickly enough to, if not avert, then at least soften the blow of an ecological crash. I tell it now for two reasons:

- Because it will be hard, for others who catch the malaise, to get the help they need to uncover its root causes. It's not easy to find therapists who in their practice make use of the findings of Maslow (and others who are part of what he called the "Third Force" in psychology). This was the case when I needed them, and it continues to be the case today. Why? The answer, according to several friends who are psychologists, is that their training focuses them almost exclusively on the non-transcendent part of our psyche. This is also why the needed help is unlikely to be found in publications by them, whether in books or blogs.

- And I tell it now because it is no longer only my story or that of a few other kindred "miners' canaries." Eco-despair may prove to be the signature malady of our time.

An online article posted by *Time* magazine is titled *In Despair Over the Polar Bear*. It begins with the story of a forty-one-year-old mother of two who "gets a stomach ache" every time she looks at a nearby volcano with a glacier at the top that has "definitely been receding over the years." It goes on to say that psychologists now have a name for her condition: "eco-anxiety, the overwhelming and sometimes debilitating concern for the worsening state of the environment. As signs of global warming accumulate, therapists say they're seeing more and more patients with eco-anxiety symptoms. Sufferers feel depression, hopelessness, and insomnia, and go through sudden, uncontrollable bouts of sobbing." [1]

Back in the early eighties there were no eco-psychologists of either the pop or the pro variety. The therapists I consulted focused on other possible reasons for my depression. The idea that we were heading for an eco-crash seemed at the time to be a far-out one, and if the threat was real there was plenty of time to do something about it. Yes we'd created environmental problems, but there were people working on them. One obvious solution to my distress was to support that work either directly, or indirectly by minimizing my contribution to those problems — insulate the house, buy recycled paper, don't drive a gas guzzler, whatever.

A possible second explanation for my angst was that I hadn't outgrown my atavistic need to stay connected with the natural world. So go hug a tree, or spend time in a nearby National Forest. But I didn't think immersions in the wilderness would help. Even looking at pictures of such places deepened my angst — they made vivid what it was that we were destroying. Contact with the natural world did once feel good, but that was to happen again only after I emerged from my gloom.

Variations of those two common sense remedies are what most eco-psychologists seem now to be selling. But if the angst is rooted in a loss of hope that we, collectively, can get off this train we are on or slow it down significantly, then these are, at best, temporary painkillers, not a cure for the ailment.

I hope this book will help you to grasp the root causes of that angst and to put together a remedy for it.

To the extent that you are not as engaged in the fight to save our habitat as you would like to be, I hope this book will help move you past a couple of the things that held me back. One was not seeing clearly enough that I had a very personal, here-and-now reason to do it.

There is a consequence of pollution and habitat destruction that is being almost totally overlooked: its impact on our psychic health. A part of us is viscerally connected to the earth, making it sick invites souls sickness. But it's easy to ascribe its symptoms — such as anger, anxiety, and depression — to other causes. What I needed — and describe here — is a way to determine the extent to which these feelings are rooted in the realm of the individual ego versus that of the more connected self.

The second thing that held me back was loss of faith in our collective ability to avert or minimize the impact of an eco-crash, whether in our lifetime or that of our now and future children. I found hope in two places: evidence that we do have what it takes to win that fight; and reasons to think we can increase the odds of doing that if we align ourselves more closely with the forces that work to maintain the health of the organism that is our biosphere.

This book also describes how a move to a more sustainable future can be catalyzed by the gifted storytellers among us, be they writers or rappers or moviemakers. If you are one of these folks and are not already engaged in that effort, I hope you will be moved to join it.

A preview of what follows

Have you caught — or are you susceptible to catching — a case of eco-malaise?

Easy question to answer if you know you are depressed about what's happening to our habitat. But what if you have caught the malady and it's in an initial mild stage that manifests itself in subtle ways, such as a general increase in irritability or impatience or feelings of unease? In hindsight I can see that this is what happened to me, and that the resulting state of mind diminished my ability to relate to people and to bring my "A" game to my work for at least a couple of years.

Even after the problem broke out into the open as a depression, it took time to figure out its cause. I knew I was bothered by what we were doing to our environment, but why wasn't that reason to be moved into action instead of into despair? To answer that question I had to first answer another: was the cause of my funk something else?

The first part of this book is an account of what I needed to do to answer those questions. It was, in essence, an exploration of what made me tick, as an individual and as a member of our species. I hope what I learned about myself will bring into sharper focus aspects of your own psyche in one or both of two ways: Yes, that's me too. No, not me, but it makes me think of something that feels more apt.

The questions I had to ask along the way were not new: Who am I, behind the face I present to others and to myself? Why do I feel as I do about my world? What do I believe the nature of things to be, and to what extent is that based on secondhand ideas? Which of those inherited ideas keep me from being at peace with my world?

Old questions, but the act of asking them helped me tailor the answers so they felt relevant to me.

Part two of this book is about imagining a way forward. OK, I understand why I feel as I do, how do I get out of this pit?

What reasons are there to think it's not too late to avert or minimize the impact of the eco-crash for which I think we are headed? How do I rekindle faith in the power of our best instincts to win the fight to save our habitat? If part of the answer is to be open to the idea that we might get an assist from the earth's equivalent of a health maintenance organization, how do I square that idea with my inner skeptic — the part of me I think of as my modern, hard-science-based sensibility? Can I see a way forward that doesn't require anyone else to do that squaring?

To find answers to these questions I had to pull together ideas about the nature of things from the viewpoints of both our scientists and traditional Native Americans. I hope going along on my excursions through those worlds will help you to create an antidote for your eco-despair, one that may or may not resemble mine.

Part I
Looking inside

1

Was the problem what it seemed to be?

> "The thing to do [is] to find out what you are really like inside, deep down, as a member of the human species, and as a particular individual."
>
> — Abraham Maslow,
> *Toward a Psychology of Being*

The first thing I did about my funk was to try to ignore it. Time mends the body, perhaps it could also heal my psyche. In the meantime get on with things as best as you can, and try to keep people from seeing that you're playing hurt. Six months went by. But the depression didn't go away, it got worse. In hindsight I wish I'd been less cavalier about it, might have saved myself a few months of pain.

My dictionary says a depression is "a condition of general emotional dejection and withdrawal; sadness greater and more prolonged than warranted by any objective reason." And to be dejected is to be "depressed in spirits, disheartened, low-spirited."

A good description of the funk I'd fallen into. A big fall for someone who had been feeling good about the way things were going for him, who used to be energized by his work, who could do sixty- hour weeks without feeling tired, who smiled often and found it easy to laugh. Now it took a lot of effort to get through the day, I felt exhausted at the end of it. And I'd lost my sense of humor.

I think I managed to keep my state of mind hidden from most people, but not from those closest to me — my wife and a few friends. They also couldn't see any cause for me to feel down. My partners and I had created a reasonably successful business. I was doing work that seemed tailor-made for me. I could get along with very diverse kinds of people. At first my friends were sympathetic, but after a while I sensed some impatience. OK, you don't like what we're doing to our world, so either do something about it, or focus on and give thanks for the fact that there's lots in your bit of it to feel good about. Get back to being the affable wise guy who was fun to be with. Snap out of this dark mood — you're beginning to scare us.

But to snap out of it I had to first understand why I was in it. Why was I unhappy? To find out I had to think, as dispassionately as I could, about my circumstances and about what I brought to them.

Unanswered questions

My friends meant well but their reaction only added another dimension to my angst. Made me feel bad about feeling bad. If there was no good reason for it, then perhaps my depression was illegitimate, something I'd made up and was holding on to for some weird or willful reason.

Yes, I was upset and angry about the way we were ravaging our environment, but why was that not reason to be moved to action rather than into despair? This was well before there was any general sense of immediacy about the consequences of the harm we were doing to it. Global warming, for example, wasn't yet seen as a here-and-now problem. Many scientists weren't convinced it was happening or, if it was, that we had a role in it. In any case it was something that might not create any serious disruptions in our way of life for decades or even generations. Plenty of time to find clever ways to modify our impact before things got out of hand. We could do something about pollution. And we could slow the rate at which we were eating up natural resources before we came close to running out of them — we'd find more efficient ways of using and replenishing them, or replace them with things of our own making. This didn't mean that there weren't issues that needed attention now, but there were specialists working on them, the rest of us didn't have to worry about them. So why was I so bummed out about them?

"Never mind why," a friend said, "you are concerned. So what if that's not the case for your friends or anyone else you know. You aren't alone, there are others out there working on some of these issues. Why don't you go help them?"

A good question. I could easily adjust my work schedule to make time for any cause I wanted to take on. In my company we encouraged people to do some pro bono work. As a partner I could probably get away with giving a third or more of my time to it. And I had something to offer: a problem-solving process that helped client teams to develop fresh ideas and to align their energies behind a course of action.

We provided two kinds of services. We gave workshops in which people learned to use our methods. We also ran meetings for our clients. At first we thought the only thing this service did was to help them get some fresh ideas in a hurry. Soon we saw that our methods also enabled them to develop consensus, to get a group of people to agree on how best to solve a problem or pursue an opportunity. It's easier to get there if in the process people build on each other's ideas instead of trying to trash them.

Many nonprofit groups had found both kinds of services useful. I had no doubt they would be helpful also to those working on environmental issues. There were several to whom I gave money. I had thought about getting in touch with them, but hadn't done it. Why not?

In my case because, well, I wasn't sure that their efforts were going to make much of a difference in the long run. We equated our high-consumption, modern lifestyle with progress and felt sorry for those in "underdeveloped" countries who didn't yet have it. Only fair to help them attain it, never mind that it was a way of life that puts us on a nasty collision course with our ecosystem.

Perhaps inspired politicians could talk us all into going on a severe diet and on having a lot fewer kids. But you and I and our kids, as consumers, account for more than two-thirds of GNP in developed countries. Shifting to a truly low-consumption lifestyle would require us to invent radically different economies. I didn't put much faith in our ability to do this in time to avert the crash. Too many people drew their power from or placed their bets for a better life on the existing system. So any work I did with the eco-warriors might help in the short-term, but it wasn't going to prevent the eventual train wreck. So why bother?

That's how I felt, though it seemed particularly inappropriate for someone like me to feel that way. Problem-solving was my profession. How many times had I said to a friend or a client that there was no such thing as a problem that couldn't be solved, given the will to do it and our capacity for ingenuity? How many times had I told the story of the rabbi who, upon hearing the scientists announce that the waters were rising and about to bring our world to an end, said to his congregation "Well, children, we got three weeks to learn to live underwater"?

Let's say I was right, there was nothing I could do to keep my dark scenario from becoming a reality. But that wasn't going to happen in my lifetime. If I couldn't put it out of my mind and enjoy life while I could, why not get to work to help future generations at least brace themselves for the crash?

What was hard to understand was why those dark thoughts had, seemingly overnight, robbed me of my old optimism and can-do spirit. My concerns about the environment had, until then, manifested themselves as a chronic but relatively low level of unease, like a mild ache in the joints that wasn't disabling and could be alleviated with an aspirin or a glass of wine.

Was the eco thing a cover-up?

Was my preoccupation with the environment a way to avoid looking at other, more personal issues? There can be many causes of a persistent depression — loss of one kind or another, problems with your work or in your relationships, sudden intimations of mortality, or a chemical imbalance in the body.

I scheduled two half-day sessions with Charles, an unconventional therapist I'd worked with before. On one occasion I spent a full week with him at his house in the woods of a small Connecticut town. A three-hour session each morning, alone time in the afternoons. Go for walks, read, think about what surfaced in the session or just let it sit. Then a one-hour evening session.

I got a lot out of that week, including a shift in perspective that led to a very positive change in my relationship with my mother. And of course Charles got a good look at me. Had he spotted anything that, though not a problem for me then, had the potential of becoming one?

Charles didn't recall anything and he saw only one thing now that might have thrown me. I had a book deal with a publisher. Two books had already been published about our problem-solving methods, both profitably.[1] Both focused primarily on the application of the methods to technical and business problems. I wanted to show how they could be used to resolve more personal issues, both at work and outside it.

I was confident I could deliver a book that people would find both useful and readable. But soon after I started writing it I got stuck. The first deadline came and went, then a second. I didn't want to quit and thought I might do better without the pressure of a deadline. So I returned the publisher's advance and told my editor I'd be back in touch when I had something to show her that I liked.

Charles suggested I might be more shaken than I realized — or wanted to admit — by my failure. I'd always delivered on every project I'd undertaken until now. This first public failure might have created a crisis of confidence that eroded my optimism, my belief that all problems were solvable. Could it be, Charles wondered, that losing confidence in myself also made me lose it in the collective abilities of my kind?

I said I'd think about it. It was true that the failure bothered me. And I didn't like how it looked to other people. Some of my colleagues, including two partners, had started to give me the kind of looks you give to someone who was once a winner but who you suspect may now have lost what it takes to be one. Didn't feel good, but my reaction was "I'll show them." I had a history of seeming to be out of a race and then coming back to win it. I hadn't given up on this one, though it was proving to be a lot harder than I'd thought it would be.

My conception of the book was simple. Its main element was examples of people using one or more of our methods to solve a variety of personal problems.

A problem is a gap between where you are and where you wish to be. You need to work on it when you run into a block on your way from here to there. What stops you from attaining your goal can be a lack of resources or know-how. It can be other people whose cooperation or blessing you need to get something done. The block can also be conceptual: you can't see a clear path to "there" from where you are standing; to see it you have to shift your viewpoint. The difficulty can also be psychological — things such as fear of failure, or a lack of confidence or motivation. The plan was to focus on both interpersonal and internal blocks.

To be persuasive my stories had to be about problems that most people cared about — I'd put together a list that my editor liked. To tell the stories convincingly the problems also had to be ones that I cared about. But the ambitions and everyday living issues that concerned most people — including, until recently, me — now seemed trivial. So the stories I forced myself to write lacked vigor and felt mechanical. I wasn't stuck in the sense that I couldn't turn out the stuff, I just didn't like what I did turn out. Well, then, why not write about my depression? Because that was a very different book and one I wasn't ready to write.

It seemed to me that I wasn't depressed because I couldn't produce a draft that worked, I couldn't produce it because I was depressed. I told Charles what I thought. I was fortunate in that he was not the kind of therapist who would say: "Aha, your resistance to my suggestion is proof of its validity." He gave me one of his long looks that made you feel you didn't have any clothes on and said "Go with your intuition — just make sure it's clean."

Was it the age thing?

> "The very frequent neurotic disturbances of adult years have this in common, that they betray the attempt to carry the psychic dispositions of youth beyond the threshold of the so-called years of discretion."
>
> — Carl Jung,
> *Modern Man in Search of a Soul*

I was forty-four. Was I bummed out about the passing of my youth? That was a "circumstance" Charles hadn't brought up and that I also hadn't thought about.

We live in a culture that worships youth. The print pages and airwaves — and now websites — are filled with images of fit young things having fun. In retrospect many of the ways in which I had fun in my twenties and thirties now seemed silly or self-destructive. But were these feelings strong enough to counter the cultural imperative to celebrate youth and mourn its passing?

Jung observes that for our ancestors "old people are almost always the guardians of the mysteries and the laws, and it is in these that the cultural heritage of the tribe is expressed. [But how] does the matter stand with us? Where is the wisdom of our old people — where are their precious secrets and visions? For the most part our old people try to compete with the young. In the United States it is almost an ideal for the father to be the brother of his son, and for the mother if possible to be the younger sister of her daughter." [2]

I knew people well past forty who pushed themselves to run or jump or slide into home base as they once did, and injured themselves because their bodies weren't as able to take the pounding. Or who partied as hard if not harder than before but refused to see that it took them a lot longer than before to recover from hangovers, and that they were demanding more of their libido than it now wanted to give.

I did some of these things too, but it seemed I did them more to be a good sport than to hang on to my youth. I'd worked hard to be who I now was, had no desire to be the less together person I was in my twenties and thirties. I spent a few weeks wondering if this was really so, if the passing of my youth was truly not a source of my angst. I couldn't smell any big whiffs of denial or self-delusion so I decided to look elsewhere for causes.

There was another possible age-related cause that I also ruled out: a heightened awareness of one's mortality. You can become obsessed by that thought by the experience, your own or of someone near to you, of a serious illness or a close brush with death. In her book Passages, Gail Sheehy describes the morbid state of mind she fell into at age thirty-five after a visit to Northern Ireland.

She took part in "a civil rights march by the Catholics of Derby." They were met, at a barricade, by British soldiers who fired tear gas shells and rubber bullets at them. The marchers retreated, she and several others to a nearby balcony. She was standing there talking to a young boy when, suddenly, real bullets started coming at them. One hit the boy and "blew his face off."

The experience threw her badly. "[A] powerful idea took hold. No one is with me. No one can keep me safe ... I had a headache for a year." [3]

I could sympathize with Sheehy but her nightmare wasn't mine, perhaps because I had no similar experience. I felt Jung spoke for me when, in talking about the midlife crisis he asks: "Is it perhaps at bottom the fear of death?" And answers that for most people "That does not seem to me very probable, because as a rule death is still far in the distance, and is therefore regarded somewhat in the light of an abstraction." Again, I had to look elsewhere for what ailed me.

I didn't schedule any more sessions with Charles or with anyone else. Instead I stumbled into a way of working on the problem on my own. I didn't make a conscious decision to take that route, it just felt like the thing to do. It proved to be the right path for me to take. But I understood this only later when I learned that psychic problems can be rooted either in the realm of the individual ego or in that of a more connected self, and that I would have been unlikely to find a therapist attuned to the second kind of problem.

If you suffer from eco-despair in either its mild or severe form, I hope this book will make it unnecessary for you to do a lot more work on it, whether with someone or on your own. But there may be occasions when for some other reason you want to do some self-analysis. So before I talk about where mine took me, I'd like to briefly note some things I learned about making the exercise productive.

Creating a vehicle for self-reflection

I was stuck in my writing project but I didn't want to stop working on it. W.C. Fields once said "If at first you don't succeed, try, try again. Then quit, no use being a damn fool about it." Was my wanting to keep at it a stubborn refusal to admit defeat? Perhaps in part, but it's also possible that at some level I knew it would provide the vehicle I needed to think about my problem on my own. If so the conscious part of me was, again, not privy to that insight.

I told my partners that I wanted to give a third of my time to my book project, and that I would take a proportional cut in pay and year-end bonuses. And that I wanted that arrangement to be open-ended. I might get done with the book in six months or I might be at it for a year or more. I didn't want a deadline. All three said fine, do it. They also said it wasn't necessary for me to take a pay cut, books about our methods were good for business. I said thanks, but let's do it my way — it would make me feel better about taking time away from the business.

Hemingway says that soon after a fighting bull enters the ring it looks for a "querencia," a place it can go to when it feels confused or under attack and needs to reassess things. It's usually a spot near the barrera from where it can face its enemies without having to worry about an attack from the rear. With my book project I had, in effect, created my querencia.

There were several ways in which the book project created the kind of space I needed to work on my problem:

- It gave me an honorable way to drop out part-time. And it gave people in my company an acceptable way to explain to clients — and to themselves — why I wasn't as available as I used to be. "He's working on a book about our stuff."
- It also allowed me to feel that I had a legitimate reason to spend big chunks of time thinking about my problem. The subject of my book was broad enough to let me feel that searching for causes of my angst was part of the work I needed to do for the project. This may not be the case for you, but doing a lot of self-reflection for its own sake would have felt like an indulgence to me.
- It added a measure of objectivity to my study of the subject. In my readings and scribblings about it, I thought not only of me but also about my likely readers, among whom I included many of my friends and colleagues.
- A dispassionate outsider's view of the situation is of course the big missing factor in any self-analysis. I couldn't fill that gap fully, but I could close it a bit. Say I read about something that could be a factor in my depression. Would that thing also create angst for any of my likely readers?
- It pushed me to put my thoughts and feelings on paper. Writing them down -- or speaking them into a voice recorder-- does two things. Putting words to your notions and emotions brings them into sharper focus. And recording them enables you to re-visit them. An idea or observation you noted a month ago often makes more sense in the light of what you've learned since then.

If you want to create a similar space for reflection, you don't have to start work on a book. It could be any project that you want to do for its own sake, but that happens to be about the human condition broadly enough to include yours. Could be exercises in writing fiction, or keeping a journal of your thoughts, or gathering material for a song album, or a play, or a series of poems.

Any project will do if it's one to which you can give regular chunks of time and one to which you can justify the giving, to yourself and, if necessary, to others. And if it's one for which you don't feel pressured to produce something to show to anyone else.

The need for a bridge

When I embarked on this leg of my book project I didn't know it was going to become a vehicle for working on my angst. It became one, but not by conscious design.

For it to become this vehicle I had to create a bridge between my problem and the subject of the book. The thinking that connected the two things was this: The book was about how to get past blocks that can keep you from solving a problem or chasing a dream. One possible block is a state of mind that leaves you with such a low level of energy that you aren't moved to do anything more than what you have to do to stay alive and maintain the appearance of being OK. It was one of many blocks and talking about it may not have a place in the book, but I'd be better able to determine that if I knew more about its causes and cures.

The connection felt tenuous but it did its job, which was to make me feel that reading and thinking about aspects of my problem was a legitimate part of the research I needed to do for the book. I needed that justification to feel OK about taking a lot of time from my business and spending it on my problem.

The bridge also helped in a couple of other ways:

- It made my exploration manageable. The general subject of depression is a vast territory and I could have got lost in the literature about the subject. But I was only poking around in a little piece of it: the possible causes of a lack of get-up-and-go energy. A small landing place but one from which I could cast a wide net. You become de-motivated because the things that used to turn you on no longer move you. Who knows something about what makes us tick? The psychologists, of course, but others — poets and novelists and historians and politicians — also know something about the subject. So I could read just about anything in my search for ideas.
- It also brought me to it with both a pragmatic and a positive mindset:
    - My reason for exploring the subject was not academic but practical — to understand what could keep us from doing the everyday things we wished to do.
    - I was looking for ideas that would enable me to say, to readers who might have run into a similar block, "You can get past it; here's some ideas that might help you to do that." (Never mind that, as I later realized, the reader I most needed to do that for was me.)

2

What I learned in the querencia

> "[It] is as if Freud supplied to us the sick half of psychology and we must now fill it out with the healthy half."
>
> — Abraham Maslow
> *Toward a Psychology of Being*

In less than two months I found the books I needed to help me understand my problem. But it took me several more months to see how the ideas in them applied to me. I often didn't see what a book by one author was trying to tell me until I came back to it after reading a book by someone else.

The authors I found most helpful were Abraham Maslow, Viktor Frankl, and William James. I recount their ideas not in the order in which I came across them, but that in which I was able to make use of them.

All three authors paint large intellectual canvases of the human psyche. What follows is not a summary of their ideas, only a description of the ones I picked out because they helped me understand what was going on in me and what I needed to do about it. I may have, in some cases, misinterpreted what they were saying, or seen something in their ideas that they didn't put there. I hope the ones I extracted from their thinking will shed light on your angst, even those that may not accurately represent what they meant to say.

We have two kinds of needs

I knew of Maslow because I'd used some of his ideas in an earlier project to produce materials for a course called *Managing for Motivation*. The materials had to make it possible to give the course without a live instructor (replaced by a "moderator" on audio tape). We were given the task by a company that was then a leading provider of such courses to the business world.*

The basic message of the course was that, as a supervisor, your attitude and behavior had an impact on the degree to which people in your team were motivated to give their best effort to their jobs. The specific behaviors the course focused on included how you listened to people, what you did with their ideas, how you dealt with differences, and how you commented on their work, both when they did it well and when they did it poorly.

We used a simplified version of Maslow's hierarchy of needs to make the case that people work hard not only to make more money or acquire power, but also to satisfy other important needs, such as those for praise, or for recognition of their competence, or for doing work that feels meaningful.

Now that I was thinking again about what does or doesn't motivate us, albeit for a very different reason, I took another look at what Maslow had to say about the subject.

We see what we are ready to see. I now found that Maslow's ideas about what makes us tick extended beyond those I'd made use of in my earlier project. There was an aspect of his picture of human nature that I had not looked at, perhaps because I didn't need to then. It was in this part

---

* The Maslow quotes in what follows are from three of his books. They are, not always in order:

(a) *Motivation and Personality*
(b) *Toward a Psychology of Being*
(c) *The Farther Reaches of Human Nature*

of the picture that I now found a plausible explanation of my angst.

In a preface to his ideas about what makes us tick, Maslow says that in his work he finds it far less useful to focus on instinctive drives or specific behaviors than on the goals they serve for the total person.

For example, he says, "sexual behavior and sexual desire [may in one individual] actually mean the desire to assure himself of his masculinity. It may in other individuals represent [a] desire to impress, or [for] closeness, friendliness, for safety, for love or for any combination of these." And, "A hysterically paralyzed arm may represent the fulfillment of simultaneous wishes for revenge, for pity, for love, and for respect."[1a]

Means and ends often form chains. "We want money so that we may have an automobile. [Which we want] because the neighbors have one and we do not wish to feel inferior to them, so that we can retain [our] self-respect [and] be loved and respected by others." It's necessary to go far enough down these chains until you get to "certain goals or needs behind which we cannot go; that is, to certain need satisfactions that seem to be ends in themselves … [The] study of motivation must be in part the study of the ultimate human goals or desires or needs."

Maslow put these ultimate goals into five categories and gave each of them a place in a hierarchy in the order of their potency. You are probably familiar with the scheme but in case you're not or need to be reminded of it here's a brief recap.

At the base of this hierarchy he put our "physiological" needs, such as those for food, water and shelter. These needs are "pre-potent," in the sense that it is difficult for any of the others to become active until these bottom-line ones are reasonably satisfied. “For the man who is extremely and dangerously hungry, no other interests exist but food [and all] capacities are put into the service of hunger-satisfaction [and capacities] that are not useful for this purpose lie dormant, or are pushed into the background. (Maslow later modified this notion that a desperately hungry person couldn’t be moved by higher needs.)

At the next higher level are the needs for “safety,” including those for “security; stability; dependency; protection; freedom from fear; [and] for structure, order, law, limits [and] so on.” Again, these needs must be met for the next higher set to emerge. An extremely insecure person “may be characterized as living almost for safety alone.”

Next come the needs for “belongingness and love.” Here, you “will feel keenly [the] absence of friends, or a sweetheart, or a [spouse], or children. [You] will hunger for affectionate relations with people in general, namely for a place in [a] group or family, [and] will strive with great intensity to achieve this goal.” You may even forget that once, when starving, you “sneered at love as unreal or unnecessary or unimportant. Now [you] will feel sharply the pangs of loneliness, of ostracism, of rejection, of friendlessness, of rootlessness.”

Once these are reasonably met, we begin to be motivated primarily by our “esteem” needs. “All people in our society (with a few pathological exceptions) have a need or desire for a stable, firmly based, usually high evaluation of themselves, for self-respect, for self-esteem, and for the esteem of others.” These needs may [be put into] two subsidiary sets.

“[First], the desire for strength, for achievement, for adequacy, for mastery and competence, for confidence in the face of the world, and for independence and freedom.

“[And] second we have [the] desire for reputation or

prestige (defining it as respect or esteem from other people), [for] status, fame and glory, dominance, recognition. attention, importance, dignity, or appreciation." He notes that these needs have been "relatively stressed by Alfred Adler and his followers, [and] relatively neglected by Freud."

At the top of the pyramid Maslow puts the need for "self-actualization." People who have "sufficiently gratified their basic needs for safety, belongingness, love, respect and self-esteem [are] motivated primarily by trends to self-actualization (defined as ongoing actualization of potentials, capacities, and talents, as fulfillment of mission (or call, fate, destiny, or vocation), as a fuller knowledge of, and acceptance of [your] own intrinsic nature, as an unceasing trend toward unity, integration or synergy within the person."[1b]

It was this last part of Maslow's picture of our nature that I now found most useful, though it was the one I'd found least interesting the first time I came across it. Back then I could relate to the bit in it about mission and vocation. That had a practical moral for the course I was working on: you can motivate the people you supervise by helping them grow professionally and, if possible, by giving them bits of work that feel meaningful to them. I knew firsthand about the impact of the work you do on your psyche. I'd quit my first job after I lost interest in it and realized this was making me snappish both at work and away from it. A big contrast with how happy I felt after I found my current line of work which, pre-funk, had indeed felt like a "mission", and I felt fortunate to have found it.

But I'd been put off by Maslow's label, "self-actualization." Made it sound too self-absorbed. Be all you can be is, as the Army ad makers know, a siren call. We like to think there is greatness locked up in us waiting to be released. But to what end? To scale those inner peaks just because they are there? That didn't feel like meaningful work.

I saw now that this was not what he was saying, and that he was aware that his term invited misunderstanding.

"The word 'self,' " he says, "seems to put people off," because it is associated with "selfish" and with "pure autonomy." But the people he is talking about are "altruistic, dedicated, [and] self-transcending." Their sense of self extends beyond their individual ego and incorporates others — not only friends and family, but all of humankind.

Once I stopped being put off by the label I could see that there were a lot of other ideas associated with it that shed light on what was going on in me.

Maslow's insights into our nature emerged from his interest in studying not only people with mental ailments but also those he deemed psychologically healthy, but who nevertheless were "by no means exempt from conflict, unhappiness, anxiety, and confusion." But their neuroses were of a different kind than those of people whose psyches were sickly. In the latter case, their suffering was caused by a "deficiency disease," for the others it was rooted in a frustration of their "growth" or "being" needs.

The "deficiency disease" has to do with unmet needs at the first four levels of the hierarchy. It is "born out of being deprived of certain satisfactions which I [call basic] needs in the same sense that water and amino acids and calcium are needs, namely that their absence produces illness." Most neuroses, he adds, involve "along with other complex determinants, ungratified wishes for safety, for belongingness and identification, for close love relationships and for respect and prestige."

In addition to these "D" or deficiency needs we also have a set of "B" or "being" needs. These reside at the uppermost level of the hierarchy and belong to the part of our being that extends beyond the boundaries of the individual ego, the part whose sense of self includes others. This self can say "I feel your pain," and mean it literally. And this merging can happen not only between mothers and their infants but between you and your tribe or nation or ecosystem.

Maslow's "healthy people" are ones who have done well enough by their lower level needs so these no longer cause them serious psychic problems. Their big problems are rooted in their "B" needs, in a failure to align their lives with their highest values and aspirations.

What are some of these needs, values, and aspirations? Because they belong to the "extended" self, many of them are other-oriented, more about giving to than taking from one's world. Among the "Motivations and Gratifications of Self-Actualizing People," Maslow includes:

- Delight in bringing about justice.
- Fighting lies and untruths.
- They try to set things right, clean up bad situations.
- They enjoy doing good.
- They don't like war but will participate in it if necessary, not if it is "an excuse for hostility, paranoia, [or] grandiosity," but for "the sake of setting things right."
- They enjoy improving things.
- They take great pleasure in their children and in helping them grow into healthy adults.
- They hate (and fight) corruption, cruelty, malice, dishonesty, pompousness, phoniness, and faking.
- They try to free themselves from illusions, to look at the facts courageously, to take away the blindfold.
- They like doing things well.[1c]

Compared with our more basic needs, these seem less tangible, more remote, things we would like to do but not ones we have to do to get on with our lives. Yet Maslow found that, once your basic needs are reasonably sated, a failure to align your life with these higher values can cause what he calls "metapathologies." These include:

- Loss of zest in life.
- Meaninglessness.
- Inability to enjoy [things]. Joylessness.
- Life ceases to be intrinsically worthwhile and self-validating.
- Apathy, resignation, fatalism.
- Sense of being useless, unneeded, of not mattering.
- Hopelessness, apathy, defeat.
- Ultimate doubt. Is anything worthwhile? Does anything matter?
- Despair, anguish, depression.
- Alienation.
- Death wishes; letting go of life. One's death doesn't matter.
- Cynicism — loss of faith in or reductive explanation of all high values.
- Spiritual illnesses and crises.

In my case life still felt like something I wanted to hang on to and I hadn't become cynical, but I'd felt everything else on the list.

Frankl's additions

> "Man's search for meaning is a primary force in his life and not a 'secondary rationalization' of instinctual drives."
>
> — Viktor Frankl[2]

About midway through my review of Maslow's ideas I started reading Viktor Frankl's book, *Man's Search for Meaning*. Its subtitle was "*an introduction to logotherapy ... a revised and enlarged version of From Death Camp to Existentialism*." Someone had given it to me three years earlier and, other than its first few pages, it had sat unread on my bookshelf. It also sat at the back of my mind on my got-to-read-sometime list.

I'd picked it up now on an impulse during a break from my research about what makes us tick. My first impression of the book had been that it was primarily about Frankl's experiences in a concentration camp. There was a part two called *Basic Concepts of Logotherapy*, but it was a heading that made it sound like an academic lecture I felt I could skip. Now I found that the ideas in it shed additional light on my problem. I bought two more of Frankl's books.[3,4]

Frankl knew Maslow; the two had commented on each other's work. They seemed kindred spirits in that they both had some nontraditional ideas about human nature, and were committed to making a case for them to the rest of us, especially those in their line of work.

Their concept of human nature was larger than that subscribed to by many others who considered themselves experts on the subject, including Freudians, Adlerians, Behaviorists, and people like the science teacher who proclaimed, to the thirteen-year-old Frankl and his classmates, that "life was nothing [more than] a combustion process, an oxidation process."[5]

They both also believed that we are not totally determined by our genes or culture or personal histories, that there is room for us to make idiosyncratic choices. We are ultimately free to choose how we face any situation, including imprisonment in a death camp.

What Frankl finds missing in Maslow's scheme is attention to our need to feel that our lives have a purpose and meaning that is unique to each of us. In Frankl's view it is both the most basic and the highest — in the sense of most encompassing — need we have. We can do a great job of satisfying all of Maslow's "D" and other "B" needs, but feel defeated by life if we don't have a "meaning to live for." And, unlike the other needs in Maslow's hierarchy the emergence of this one does not require "lower" needs to be reasonably satisfied. He saw that in fact it can "become most urgent" when lower ones are suffering great deprivation, as in the deliberately brutal and dehumanizing concentration camps (including Auschwitz and Dachau) of which he was a survivor.

His experience in the camps convinced him that we had the ability to create meaning even in the most severe conditions. And, that this ability had survival value. There was no doubt in his mind that it increased your odds of physically surviving those conditions or, if you didn't, of going to your death with some measure of equanimity and dignity. Many of his fellow inmates were sustained by the thought that they needed to survive to bear witness to the horror, to ensure that the world heard about it. That, at that time, was the meaning of their lives.

After the war Frankl began to see more clearly the other side of the coin. In the victorious West, especially America, you could be living in what seemed the best of times, be doing well socially and financially, and still be driven to despair and suicide if you felt there was no meaning to your life.

Frankl also came to believe that, because it has survival value, our ability to find meaning in any situation or encounter is innate, part of our evolutionary inheritance.

I read only a few of Maslow and Frankl's numerous publications. Enough to get what I needed from my virtual therapy sessions with them, but certainly not enough to do a defendable dissertation about where their ideas did or did not mesh. But it seemed to me that Maslow's ideas were not as incongruous with Frankl's as the latter sometimes said they were.

Maslow didn't give the need for meaning its own space in his hierarchy, above the other five or alongside one of them. But in a table in which he lists "B" values and the "Metapathologies" that result from their "deprivation" he includes in the first column "Meaningfulness" and in the second that corresponds with it, "Meaninglessness, Despair, Senselessness of life."[1c] And after reading one of Frankl's papers Maslow agrees with him that the "will to meaning" is to be regarded as our "primary concern."

And they were both convinced that part of our intrinsic nature is a "transcendent" self that is not confined by the boundaries of the personal ego and includes in itself others. Here, Frankl goes further by saying that you can create meaning only when you are moved by your transcendent self, that is, by the needs of someone other than you or by the need to serve some cause more important to you than your own wellbeing. But even this is an assertion I think Maslow would have endorsed.

He says of his "self-actualizers" that "All such people are devoted to some task, call, vocation, beloved work... [Some] cause outside oneself and bigger than oneself, something not merely selfish, something [in that sense] impersonal ... One gets the feeling of a beloved job, [and] of something for which [they are] a 'natural,' something [they're] suited for, [that is right for them], even something [they were] born for."

What Frankl helped bring into sharp focus was that I too once had a beloved job, work that didn't feel like work because I had a predisposition for it. Work that felt meaningful because I was helping people solve problems and giving them thinking tools that helped them tap the creative side of their minds.

What I hadn't seen clearly until now was that when I stopped feeling that way about my work I'd lost not only a beloved job but that which gave a sense of purpose and meaning to my life. Frankl was saying this was a very big loss, and that mourning it was what a chunk of my angst was about. Felt right.

Who, me?

Was it possible that Maslow and Frankl were right, that my funk was caused by the emergence of a larger self and my failure to acknowledge and attend to its needs? If I listened to my gut the answer was a loud yes.

After all these years (over two decades) I can recall clearly my reaction when my virtual sessions with Maslow and Frankl brought me to the point where their explanation of my angst began to seem like a real possibility. I was in my office, the door shut and wearing its "Don't disturb" sign. A feeling of relief flowed through me. I felt elated. I couldn't stay in my chair, had to get up and walk around in my office.

If this was true then — hallelujah! — my problem was legit, I wasn't feeling the way I did because I was a weirdo. If you recall, I'd been feeling bad about feeling bad — given my fortunate circumstances I thought I had no right to be depressed. Maslow and Frankl were saying that there were other reasons for me to feel bad and that, in fact, I had cause to feel good about feeling that way because the pain was part of a process of psychic growth. The lightening of my mood made me see how much I'd been weighed down by the sense that my angst was not legitimate.

Maslow had given me a way to settle the question of whether or not what felt like eco-despair was a cover-up for other issues in my life. Instead of looking haphazardly for things in my past and present that might be causing me grief, I could look more methodically at possible sources in each of his need types.

His "B" needs were those of the part of us that transcends the boundaries of the personal ego and is thus viscerally connected with its world. The "D" needs belong to the part that thinks of itself primarily as an individual being connected only circumstantially to the rest of creation.

I saw that I had deficiencies at all the "D" need levels above the physiological, but none felt serious enough to explain my depression. Maslow was saying that this didn't have to mean I was fooling myself about that because a frustration of those needs wasn't the only source of angst.

Perhaps my sense of self had begun to include in it the natural world. If so, then it was reasonable for me to be bummed out by and furious about what we were doing to it. Feeling that way may even be built into our genes. If it's true that the wellbeing of our species depends on the health of our ecosystem then concern for it would, over time, become embedded in our nature. Here I was extending Maslow's and Frankl's notions of the transcendent self beyond where they might have wanted to take it. In their references to it they seemed to extend its boundaries to include only others of our kind. But I thought my further extension of it was something that would not have displeased them.

There were other reasons why I felt relieved:

- I now had a plausible handle on my problem, or at least a part of it. It's unsettling to not have any clue about what ails you.
- It was comforting to hear that the problem wasn't peculiar to me, that it was rooted in the nature of

my kind. The specifics may be different, but there were others who, like me, were struggling with issues created by the emergence of their "B" needs. The idea that you are not alone in your suffering lessens the pain.

- Maslow's ideas also helped me deal with something else that had been bothering me. I had stopped being energized by the idea of making a lot of money, for myself or for the business, and I'd felt that this was somehow unmanly. If his diagnosis was right I had no cause to feel bad about it. I had "sufficiently satisfied" my need to feel competent in that way, and was moving on to fight other battles. Again, it was only after I saw why I didn't need to feel bad about it that I realized how much I'd been bothered by it.

Yes, but. That the contact with Maslow's and Frankl's ideas had lifted my spirits meant that at some level I believed they were the right explanation for a big chunk of my problem. But I hadn't yet learned to trust my feelings, hadn't figured out how to tell when they spoke the truth and when they didn't. (Gotten better at it, but still far from all the way there.) So I needed my head to validate my "aha" reaction.

Were Maslow's ideas appealing because it flattered me to think I was one of his "self-actualizers," a select group of folks who lived on a higher plane than the average person? Did I really belong in that club? These seemed to be very evolved people in the sense of having moved beyond their "D" needs. I could see many ways in which I was still stuck there.

For example, I was easily offended and hurt when my colleagues did things that showed a lack of appreciation for the big contribution to the company's coffers that was made by the *Managing for Motivation* package that I'd developed (with much help from one of the people who gave us that job, but little more than administrative help from any members of our staff).

I was also upset by their failure to grasp how hard it had been for me to learn to produce those kinds of materials. This despite my knowing that the skills involved were not obvious and not easily inferred from the finished package. They were not unlike those required to write computer software, all but invisible to the uninitiated. It was not reasonable to expect my colleagues to see that I'd acquired them, yet I was bothered by their not applauding me for having done that.

There were other signs of a needy ego. Any time two or more people get together each of them brings to the encounter at least two agendas. One is overt: at work it may be to resolve a dispute or to find a fresh approach to a persistent old problem; in social settings it could be to keep your connections alive or to have a good time together.

The other, usually unconscious agenda, is to look good — whether physically (sure is in great shape for her age) or psychically (wow, what a witty or clever or knowledgeable or contained or serene person). There may be other hidden agendas (such as steering people to conclusions you want them to make), but there are always also the first two. I became aware of the looking good or "ego" agenda after watching hundreds of videotapes of business meetings.

We are thinking animals, we identify with our minds and with the products of our minds — our ideas and insights and opinions about things. So one of the most common ways people play the ego-agenda game is by trying to show you that their mind is sharper than yours. One cheap (in the sense of least effort) way is to poke holes in your ideas (I'm smarter than you if I can spot the fatal flaws in them). The game can be played offensively (grabbing the podium, attacking ideas), or defensively (arguing your point, setting the stage before airing an idea, not voicing any thoughts that might get trashed or sound ill-informed).

As a facilitator it's fatal to play such games with the people in your session. One of the things that made me effective in this role was that I was able to avoid them in that milieu. Which made it more culpable when I found myself playing them in social and family settings.) In most instances I was more aware than the people I was with of the existence of these games and of how you could get drawn into them. And yet I did get drawn into them, often enough to feel that my ego was a lot needier than I wanted it to be.

I was also having problems in my marriage and with my partners at work. (Both those relationships would soon end, reasonably amicably.) Given that I clearly hadn't "sufficiently satisfied" all these "D" needs, how could my "B" needs have become active enough to be the cause of my distress?

The question arose because I had trouble hearing Maslow's answer, which was that the two kinds of needs can co-exist:

> [Our discussion of] these five sets of needs [may give] the false impression that a need must be satisfied 100 percent before the next [higher one] emerges. In actual fact, most members of our society who are normal are partially satisfied [and] partially unsatisfied in all their basic needs at the same time. [If] I may assign arbitrary figures for the sake of illustration, the average [person] is satisfied perhaps 85 percent in [the] physiological needs, 70 percent in [the] safety needs, 50 percent in [the] love needs, 40 percent in [the] self-esteem needs, and 10 percent in [the] self-actualization needs.[1a]

He also has a section titled "The Imperfections of Self-actualizing People," in which he says about them:

> Our subjects show many of the lesser human failings. They too are equipped with silly, wasteful, or thoughtless habits. They can be boring, stubborn, irritating. They are by no means free [from] superficial vanity [and pride]. Temper outbursts are not rare.[1a]

My problem was that it was hard to keep these things in mind given the glowing picture of these people he paints ninety-nine percent of the time. He says, for example, that his "investigations on self-actualization [started out] as the effort of a young [student] to understand two of his teachers whom he loved, adored, and admired and who were very, very wonderful people. [I could] not be content simply to adore them but sought to understand why these two people were so different from [most others].

"They were remarkable human beings. My training in psychology equipped me not at all for understanding them. It was as if they were not quite people but something more than people."

Maslow began to look at them more thoughtfully and recorded his observations. And then, he says, there came a point in this attempt to understand them when "I realized in one wonderful moment that their two patterns could be generalized. I was talking about a kind of person, not about two noncomparable individuals. There was wonderful excitement in that. I tried to see whether this pattern could be found elsewhere, and I did find it elsewhere, in one person after another."[1c]

He found it in people he knew, and he thought he saw it in many public figures. Among the "highly probable" ones he includes Einstein, Schweitzer, Spinoza, Jane Addams, William James, and Aldous Huxley. Some club, and the last two were writers I admired and had put on high pedestals.

These examples and his many lists of the characteristics and qualities of self-actualizing people created an image of them beside which his occasional qualifications seemed written in very fine print, easy to overlook. For some weeks I continued to have trouble accepting his diagnosis, even as a working assumption. Until my eye fell on the spine of a book on my shelves, *Lame Deer, Seeker of Visions* subtitled 'the Life of a Sioux Medicine Man'.[6]

Sure, I'd put him in that club. And then I remembered that he talks in the book about how as a young man he chased women and went on drinking binges, the last a dangerous thing for an Indian to do, especially back then.

> The white police around here like to work Mister Indian over just because he is a little drunk, cusses a little bit. So they pound him, and because he's drunk he feels nothing. They mash him up, hurt him bad. Sometimes the Indian dies; sometimes he comes out of it with a fractured skull or a cut mouth. He is drunk and can't fight back. We have some undersized policemen, skinny little good-for-nothing lightweights, who use their guns, irons, clubs and saps to hit the 'big tough Indian.' It makes them feel like men.

One night, Lame Deer says, he "had a few too many [but] I wasn't really drunk, just a bit unsteady, friendly like, and in a mood for fun. But they arrested me all the same, pushing and manhandling me." He tries to joke his way out of it but one of the cops spits an epithet at him and hits him hard with a sap. Lame Deer hits him back and knocks him down. There are three cops and they pin him down, the one he'd hit sitting on his chest. He has a heavy carved silver ring on his finger, "and he smashed it again and again into my face while his two buddies held me down. [Well], he smashed the bone under my eye, really splintered and crumbled it. Finally his arm got tired and I passed out."

He wakes up in a hospital. "I guess they worried about word getting out about what they had done to me." The doctor tells him he's OK, "except for a little bruise. You must have fallen down when you was drunk."

He is now a healer, is considered a holy man. It's many years later but the "guy with his big silver ring" is still around, and every time he sees him "my cheek begins to hurt." And the thought comes to his mind, "Maybe I should get even, but my inner voice says no." There's a struggle. "One voice tells me: 'Don't be a hero, that's not in your line. You're a healer, not a hurter.' But another voice [says]: 'Be a man!' Maybe one of these days, when that old cheek is acting up again, I'll get mad. Soon I'll be too old to take a good swing at somebody, but when I'm mad I feel thirty years younger."

Two morals of the story for me. One, that you may at some stage feel you have little in common with folk you consider heroic, but that doesn't mean you can't evolve in their direction. And two, that even when you get there, not all your thoughts and acts are aligned with your highest values and aspirations. Getting them aligned is a lifelong task. You can start working on it at any stage of your development.

Perhaps all people held in high esteem should squeal on themselves. It would help us see that they weren't born that way; they had to struggle to get there. We'd be less awed by them, more inspired to be the best that we can be.

Thinking about Lame Deer helped me to accept the idea that the way out of my funk was to get going on the task of aligning the way I lived with my "B" values and aspirations. But there was a difficulty.

It seemed to me that there were several parts to the task:

- Engage in activities that aim to make things better in some part of my world. Things that, in Bob Dylan's words, "serve somebody."
- Live in a way that is socially and environmentally responsible.

- And, work on my state of mind. The more free I became of inner conflicts and tensions and anxieties the more effective I was likely to be in doing the first two things.

I could see ways in which I could go about the second and third tasks, but had trouble with the first.

There are of course many ways to "serve somebody." Doing what you can to give your children a head start in their lives. Caring for an ailing parent or spouse. Community work. Donating your expertise as a doctor or lawyer or business manager or mediator. Creating music or books or movies or paintings that feed our best and not our worst instincts. Whatever.

My difficulty arose because I didn't have kids of my own or any other family members I needed to look after. The only work I could think of that felt meaningful to me was doing something about the ecological train wreck I saw coming. And this brought me back to my old impasse. I wasn't moved to do anything because I didn't feel it would make any difference; it wouldn't alter the outcome.

Understanding grows in spirals. I was back to my old "what's the use" question, but I was looking at it from a different point of view because I now knew more about what might be going on in me. I could see more of the territory in which I lived and in that sense I was looking at it from a higher elevation. This made me more ready to explore a way out of my impasse that I came across in a book by the American psychologist and philosopher, William James.

Before I go on to say more about that path I'd like to close this chapter by addressing two other questions related to the task of aligning the way you live with your "B" values and aspirations.

To what extent should you work on this task on your own versus with a therapist?

Working on issues related to a mix of our "B" and "D" needs can be a lifelong task. At some point you may wonder whether it's best to do the work on your own or with the help of a "pro. If so, here are some things you may want to keep in mind.

Maslow affirmed my choice of self-analysis. If my problem was indeed rooted in my "B" needs then, according to him, I'd been right to make that my mode of therapy. Why?

Because interpersonal therapy, that is, one in which you work with another person, is necessary if your problem arises from unmet "D" needs. The big deficits in most such cases are ones that can only be supplied by others — the need to feel safe with them, and to be accepted, or loved, or valued and esteemed by them. Because these are in essence interpersonal problems, they are best worked on that way, with another person. However:

"[In most cases] therapy must be interpersonal. But this fact has been badly over-generalized." By this he means that it is usually assumed, by people who need help and by those from whom they seek it, that it is always the best option for looking inside. But this is not so. "[It] is unwise, he says, "to forget that frequently the problems and conflicts of [growth motivated people] are solved by [them] turning inward in a meditative way, i.e., self-searching rather than seeking for help from someone … [Many] of the tasks of self-actualization are largely intrapersonal …"[1b]

I don't think Maslow was saying that if you're such a person you must go it alone. Many of his patients belonged to that group, and he was able to help them. I think he was saying that, back then, the odds were very low that you would find someone who recognized your problem.

Maslow was part of a relatively small group of psychologists he called the "Third Force" — those who believed the Freudians and Adlerians and Behaviorists were so focused on some aspects of human nature that they couldn't see the whole beast.

But I'm sure there are many more of them now, so your odds of finding a "Maslow" or a "Frankl" are much better. The odds are even higher if you are clear about who you're looking for:

Someone who knows about and believes in the existence of both your "D" and your "B" needs and can therefore help you decide which ones are key in your case. Someone who agrees with Maslow (and Frankl) that in the "B" values lies "the meaning of life for most people, but [many don't] recognize that they have these metaneeds." And that "part of the counselor's job may be to make them aware of these needs in themselves, just as the classical psychoanalyst [made] people aware of their instinctoid basic [i.e., "D"] needs."

How best to use your talents and abilities to do your bit for your world?

Sometimes the answer is to find a different way to make a living. Here's an example from a public radio program, *The Story*. The host, Dick Gordon, is talking to a woman, Jo Holt. She describes how she quit her job as an engineer building high-tech weapons for the Defense Department and became a nurse. She realized she needed to do something different for a living after she was congratulated for successfully finishing an assignment, and woke up to the fact that the bits of technology she had helped to create were used ultimately to improve ways of killing people in battle.

She wasn't going to be pulling any triggers, and there may be times when there were good reasons for others to pull them. But it didn't feel right to be doing that work, didn't sit well with her conscience. So she changed careers, though it was not easy to do.

But it isn't always necessary to change your job if the one you're doing doesn't feel sufficiently meaningful. If you don't think the goods and services you help provide are harmful, it may make sense to keep doing it to make a living and supplement it with other activities that fill the void. What made this hard for me to do, once I regained hope, was the tendency to look for one solution that would satisfy both sets of needs — for money and for doing something that made me feel I was "serving somebody." It's often easier to do both things if you unbundle the solution. I learned this from "Jim," a participant in one of my creative problem-solving courses.

Jim worked in a manufacturing plant. He was a first-line supervisor, a position at the dividing line between hourly workers and the salaried ranks of "managers." During a break on the second day of the course Jim said he liked some of the problem solving tools I'd introduced.

"I can use them in the work I do after hours with physically handicapped kids," he said.

"What about in your job, your regular work?" I asked.

"Yeah, there too," he said, "but the other thing is my real work. The job is a good way to support my family, the company is ethical and takes a lot of trouble to make the plant a safe place for us to work in. I try to do a good job, I'm glad to have it. But it's what I do after hours and on weekends that really matters to me."

Some of his peers dreamed of someday becoming a plant manager. But Jim had no wish to climb that ladder. "The higher you go," he said, "the more call there is on your time beyond the regular hours." It was a price he was not willing to pay, and he seemed very much at peace with that decision. I also know a few lawyers, physicians, and other professionals who have made analogous decisions, and who all seem to have found a degree of equanimity by making them.

3

Ways out of the impasse

> "At the bottom [our whole concern] is with the manner of our acceptance of the universe. Do we accept it only in part and grudgingly, or heartily and altogether? Shall [we] think that even with [the evil we see], there are ways of living that must lead to good? If we accept the whole, shall we do so as if stunned into submission, [or] shall we do so with enthusiastic assent?"
>
> — William James
> *The Varieties of Religious Experience*

I became a William James fan after I read his two-volume set, *The Principles of Psychology*. I read the books because he had sections in them about things related to my work, such as the mental process involved in an act of imagination, and the virtues of thinking by analogy. I liked the way he thought about things.

He looked at them from many angles and his ideas emerged not from theory but from observations of real events. And the goal of his reflections was pragmatic — to arrive at ideas that could be put to use in everyday life. The style of the writing was old-fashioned but the ideas remained valid and thought provoking.

I collect books. When I find one I want to add to my shelves, I look for and buy others by the same author. Some get read right away, others a lot later. I had a half dozen of James's books in my collection.

In my querencia, when I took breaks from my writing and wanted to read something, I usually picked whatever book I was drawn to, regardless of whether it seemed related to my task. That's how I found myself reading James's *Essays on Faith and Morals*. And came across a way of thinking about my impasse that wouldn't have occurred to me. There is, said James, a kind of "*tedium vitae*" that is not rooted in "organic sources," but is a form of pessimism and funk that is "essentially a religious disease."[1]

I have a problem with the "r" word, but James made it possible for me to stay with his thought by making it clear that to him being religious had nothing to do with adherence to the tenets of any particular religion. It meant only "faith in the existence of an unseen order of some kind in which the riddles of the natural [world] may be found explained." That order may include in it only some universal principles, but no deity. James's preference was for one that included both.

James also says that an inner conflict arises for those in whom there is not only a strong need to believe in this unseen order but also "an ingrained naturalism and materialism of mind which can only admit facts that are actually tangible. Of this sort of mind the entity called 'science' is the idol. Fondness for the word 'scientist' is one way you may know its votaries."

I wouldn't have called myself a "votary" of science, but I did have degrees in physics and engineering. I had a mixed reaction to the idea that I might have a need to believe in James's unseen order. Despite his assurance that this didn't mean a hankering for "religion" in the usual sense of the word, the idea felt problematic.

I was a happy agnostic, content to sit on the fence and

pat myself on the back for being more skeptical than the believers, but more open-minded than the atheists. I didn't want to get off that comfortable seat and step into what felt like brambly territory. The notion of an unseen order that housed some Power for good raised questions I wasn't sure I wanted to tackle. Such as:

How could such a Being have come to be? Was this Intelligence there before the Big Bang or did it evolve afterward? Was there only one Cosmic Being or also other more local Intelligences associated with the One? As far as we are concerned, is that One benevolent, malevolent, or indifferent? If such a Power cares about us, how come there is so much misery and pain and violence in our world?

I was reluctant to walk into this terrain. I wasn't interested in getting into a debate with myself about such things if the only reasons for doing so were primarily philosophical and not practical. But I had a hard time dismissing James's diagnosis as a factor in my angst, even though it wasn't clear how it created a need for me to believe in something like his unseen order.

I found the answer to that question in another of James's books, *The Varieties of Religious Experience.*[2]

"Varieties" is a big book. What follows includes only a few bits of it, those relevant to my question. So the narrative in which they are embedded is mine, not that of James. When you pluck things out of one story and plump them into another their meaning and flavor can change. If you are a James scholar you may find instances of this in what follows. We take from others what we need to take from them and in the process are prone to tailor their ideas to our ends.

The need for an antidote

James says, in essence, that we all need an antidote to our knowledge that all is not well with our world, that evil exists, and that much of what is wrong is the doing of our own dark side. Even if nothing bad has happened to us personally, we can't not be aware of the bad things that happen to others.

If we don't have an antidote, we become "sick souls." Pessimism creeps into our bones. We become susceptible to despair and cynicism, we lose our ability to love, we lose hope, we question whether life is worth living.

How we respond to our awareness of the dark side depends on our conception of the nature of things. We all have, James says, "a sense of [the] cosmos as an everlasting presence, intimate or alien, terrible or amusing, lovable or odious." This sense is based on our intuitions about and experiences of the world, as well as on ideas about it that we absorb from others. It is created, for the most part, by a process that is "involuntary and inarticulate and often half unconscious." However we come by them, our ideas about "the character of this universe in which we dwell" make us "either strenuous or careless, devout or blasphemous, gloomy or exultant, about life at large."

Our sense of the universe may or may not include ideas in it that we can use to create an effective antidote — one that sustains our spirit, that enables us to make our peace with our world, or at least to "think that even with the evil, there are ways of living that must lead to good." And the ideas that work for one person may not work for another.

James says that there are, in this regard, two kinds of people. There are those who acquire an antidote that works for them early in life and that continues to work for them thereafter. Such people need to be "born" only once — they do not need to change their ideas about the universe and in this sense enter or be "born again" into a new conception of it.

The other kind are people who do need to be "twice-born" because they either never acquired an effective antidote, or because the one they did acquire worked for a while and then lost its power. I was clearly in this last category. The cocktail of ideas that used to sustain my spirit didn't do that now. I needed to create a new one or at least to add some new ideas into the old mix.

Antidote options

The obvious cure is of course belief in the existence of some power for goodness that is strong enough to give us at least even odds of someday winning the fight against the dark side.

No deities need be involved. The faith can be in ourselves, in the collective power of all the people on earth who are good, who are actively engaged in the fight on some front — against some specific injustice, for example, or against some of the conditions that produce poverty or hunger or disease or nasty dictators. You don't need to believe that the good people outnumber the bad, or that they ever will, only that their numbers are growing and that once their fraction exceeds some critical threshold, the balance will be tipped in their favor and they will start to gain ground on the enemy.

Some people acquire this faith largely unconsciously, perhaps by being exposed to good people early in life. Others have to think their way to it. It took Maslow many years of research to convince himself that each of us has "an essential biologically based inner nature [that is not] intrinsically evil, but rather neutral or positively good." And, "What we call evil behavior [is most often] a secondary reaction to frustration of this intrinsic nature." Whether our good or our bad impulses dominate depends on the conditions in which we live. There is hope for us because we have the smarts we need to improve those conditions for steadily increasing numbers of people.

This faith can rest on a feeling of confidence in our kind, per se. Or it can be based on confidence in some of our creations, such as Science or Art or the Free Market or Capitalism or Socialism or Democracy. Or on confidence in our ability to win a specific fight, for example, that we can find a cure for some disease, or restore the rights of a specific group of disenfranchised people.

It was faith in our kind that had kept me from being overwhelmed by my awareness of the existence of evil. I was a child living in India when the country gained its independence and was split into two (one secular and the other, Pakistan, a religious state). A lot of ethnic butchery took place at the time.

We lived in the Punjab, one of the two states (the other was Bengal) in which most of it was done. By some estimates more than a million people were killed and 25 million displaced, the latter almost nine percent of the population, at that time, of a little over 300 million.

Even as a very young person you couldn't avoid hearing about the nastiness being indulged in by a lot of people, Muslims on the one side, Hindus and Sikhs on the other. Some of the victims as well as the perpetrators were people we knew.

But in our immediate circle, family and friends, there were people (Hindus, Muslims, and Sikhs) who never faltered in the view that the "others" were family, and in many cases saved their lives at great risk to their own. All of these people believed that ultimately our better nature would prevail. And they all believed that education and science would help us eliminate the conditions — such as wretched poverty and unthinking prejudice — that prevented this better nature from emerging.

Perhaps because of this history I had no trouble accepting Maslow and Frankl's ideas of our higher nature. I'd seen that nature at work, though it hadn't occurred to me that the examples I'd seen said something not only about those people but also about our kind. But despite this confirmation I'd lost faith in my kind.

The "evil," in my case, was our ravaging of our ecosystem and our refusal to see the great dangers it posed for our own welfare. There were some good people fighting to stop or at least slow down the rate of destruction, but I didn't think their efforts were going to ward off those dangers. (I felt, you may recall, that our way of life had put us on a high-speed train headed for a nasty crash. We were too wedded to its course to change it because we equated it with progress and the good life. And because too many people drew their power from or vested their hopes for a better life on our current path.)

James was suggesting that, if I couldn't rekindle this faith, I was left with two options. One was to replace that faith with belief in some power for good other than ours. The second was to find a way to live with my disillusionment and the sense of hopelessness that accompanied it.

James describes three strategies for living with it. He doesn't think any of them do as much for the spirit as belief in some other power for good. This latter route was open for me because I was not totally closed to the idea that such a power might exist. But you may find it harder to entertain that idea, so I'll talk first about the other option. Despite what James considers to be the shortcomings of the three ways of pursuing it, each of them has elements in it that can be used to deal with some of the challenges of daily living.

Living with it

Two of the three ways of living in a world in which there is no power bigger than ours, or none that you can trust, are ones practiced and named by the Old Greeks. They were likely used by others before them, and continue to be used today. They are:

Stoicism — The philosophy that urges us, says my dictionary, to be "free from passion, unmoved by joy or grief, and [to] submit without complaint to unavoidable necessity." James adds that the Stoic "insensibility" is driven by the idea that "The only genuine good that life can yield [us] is the free possession of [our] soul; all other goods are lies."

Epicureanism — As James puts it, "The Epicurean said: 'Seek not to be happy, but rather to escape unhappiness; strong happiness is always linked with pain; therefore hug the safe shore, and do not tempt the deeper raptures. Avoid disappointment by expecting little, and by aiming low; and above all do not fret.'" (My dictionary gives the more common definition of the epicure: "a person who cultivates a refined taste, as in food, art, music, etc.," or someone "given or adapted to luxury or indulgence in sensual pleasures.")

How effective are these approaches to the problem? James doesn't give them high marks.

"The early Greeks," he says,

> are continually held up to us in literary works as models of [the] joyousness which the religion of nature may engender. There was indeed much joyousness among the Greeks — Homer's enthusiasm for most things that the sun shines upon is steady. But even in Homer the reflective passages are cheerless, and the moment the Greeks grew systematically pensive and thought of ultimates, they became unmitigated pessimists. The jealousy of the gods, the

> nemesis that follows too much happiness, the all-encompassing death, fate's dark opacity, the ultimate and unintelligible cruelty, were the fixed background of their imagination. [Their] beautiful joyousness [is] only a poetic fiction.

"Stoic insensibility and Epicurean resignation," James adds, "were the farthest advance which the Greek mind made" in developing antidotes to its awareness of evil. "There is dignity in both these forms of resignation ... [But] they leave the world in the shape of an un-reconciled contradiction, and seek no higher unity."

What about some of the ideas Plato has about the origins and nature of a first-cause God and the secondary gods associated with him? The first Creator, he says in the Timaeus dialogue, "was good [and] desired that all things should be good and nothing bad, so far as this was attainable."

My guess is that James makes no mention of such ideas because he was a pragmatist, and he saw no practical answers in them about how to live with our awareness of evil other than those of the Stoic and the Epicure.

I could see how elements of both those philosophies could make good medicine in some situations, as when someone has to live with a severe disability, or is faced with a slow and painful but certain death. I know people who managed their terminal illnesses admirably — calmly, with great dignity and courage and, in the best sense of the word, stoically.

But the idea of adopting either one as a general stance toward life didn't appeal to me. I wasn't ready to give up on the possibility that there were some powers for good other than our own. Perhaps I wouldn't succeed in convincing the skeptic in me that they could exist, and then something like stoic resignation might be the only option. But I'd just begun to entertain that idea, too soon to tell how far I could take it.

Averting the gaze — The third strategy, James says, is to acknowledge the existence of the dark side of things but choose to focus on the bright side, on the full half of the glass. Some people, seem to be born with this sunny view of the world; others have to work to create and maintain it.

"[We] all know someone," James says, "perhaps more [often] young than old, whose soul is of this sky-blue tint, whose affinities are rather with flowers and birds and all enchanting innocencies than with dark human passions, who can think of no ill of man or God."

It's also possible to cultivate this state of mind, for example, by learning to exercise a zen-like control over where your thoughts dwell. It is, James says, a "deliberately optimistic scheme of life," one that directs us to "settle [our] scores with the more evil aspects of the universe by systematically declining to lay them to heart or to make much of them, by ignoring them in [our reflections.]" And you can justify this stance thus: "Evil is a disease and worry over disease is itself an additional form of disease, which only adds to the original complaint." So by ignoring it you are helping to diminish its potency.

For James, the "supreme contemporary example of such an inability to feel evil" was Walt Whitman who, he says, "owes his importance in literature to the systematic expulsion from his writings of all contractile elements. The only sentiments he allowed himself to express were of the expansive order; and he expressed [these] vicariously for all [his readers], so that passionate and [mystic] emotion suffuses his words, and ends by persuading the reader that men and women, life and death, and all things are divinely good.

"Thus it has come about that many persons today regard Walt Whitman as the restorer of the eternal natural religion. He has infected them with his own love of comrades, with his own gladness that he and they exist. [He] is even explicitly compared with the founder of the Christian religion, not altogether to the advantage of the latter."

But, James says, Whitman is not "your mere [natural] man who has not tasted of the tree of good and evil. He is aware enough of sin for a swagger to be present in his indifference towards it, a conscious pride in that [stance]."

"[Whitman's] optimism is too voluntary and defiant; his gospel has a touch of bravado and an affected twist, and this diminishes its effect on many readers who yet are well disposed towards optimism, [and are] quite willing to admit hat in important respects [he] is of the genuine lineage of prophets."

The temptation to swagger aside, what else is wrong with averting the gaze as a strategy for dealing with your awareness of the dark side of things?

At first glance, "deliberately [excluding] evil from your field of vision [may] seem a difficult feat to perform for one who is intellectually sincere [and] honest about facts." But, "the situation is too complex to lie open to so simple a criticism."

In part this is because holding on to an optimistic, hopeful view of life has its practical uses. It can lend strength to the processes the body uses to heal itself. It can help "the halt to walk [and] life-long invalids to [have] their health restored." It can also help you deal with setbacks and disappointments — losing a race, a job, a business, a fortune, a friendship.

But though focusing on the good aspects and possibilities of your life can help you deal with personal misfortunes, it doesn't solve the deeper problem: it doesn't fortify you against your awareness of the dark side of the universe.

As James puts it,

> To begin with, how can things so insecure as the successful experiences of this world afford a stable anchorage? [In] the healthiest and most prosperous existence, how many links of illness, danger, and disaster are always interposed? Unsuspectedly from the bottom of every fountain of pleasure [something] bitter rises up: a touch of nausea. a falling dead of the delight, a whiff of melancholy, things that sound a knell, for fugitive as they may be, they bring a feeling of coming from a deeper region and often have an appalling convincingness. The buzz of life ceases at their touch as a piano-string stops sounding when the damper falls upon it.
>
> Of course the music can commence again — and again and again — at intervals. But with this the [deliberately sunny] consciousness is left with an irremediable sense of precariousness. It is a bell with a crack; it draws its breath on sufferance and by an accident.
>
> Even if we suppose [some] to be so packed with [sunny-mindedness] as never to have experienced in their own person any of these sobering intervals, still, if [they are] reflecting [beings they] must generalize and cast [their] lot with that of others, and, doing so, [must] see that [their] escape is just a lucky chance and no essential difference. [They] might just as well have been born to an entirely different fortune. And then indeed the hollow security! What kind of frame of things is it of which the best you can say is, 'Thank God, it has let me off clear this time!' Is not its blessedness a fragile fiction?

Though James doesn't say so, he would likely have agreed that a sunny-minded person is not always someone "whose optimism is too voluntary and defiant." I've known people for whom that stance toward the world seems to be not something assumed but an outcome — they have found a way, consciously or unconsciously, to make their peace with their world, and they feel happy about that.

This could be the case for those who feel they are doing things that serve the needs of something or someone other than themselves. I used to be one of those people.

I wasn't sunny-minded in the sense of being someone "whose soul is of [a] sky-blue tint," but I was generally optimistic; my stance toward most any problem was one of confidence that it could be solved. I felt good about things much of the time. If asked why I wouldn't have known what to say. But when I read what Maslow had to say about our "B" needs I saw that satisfying the need to do something for a cause larger than yourself releases good feelings. In my case I felt I was helping individuals and institutions to find more productive or satisfying ways of doing things, and I hadn't yet lost my faith in Homo Sap.

The "sunny" people you come across may not be putting it on; they may be feeling inclined kindly towards others and themselves because they're doing something that seems worthwhile to them. They may not think this way about that "work," they may be doing it because it comes easy or just feels like the thing to be doing.

For people who have to tend to their "B" needs, not having a measure of sunny-mindedness is an indication that there is a disconnect between these needs and the way they are living.*

* Our "B" or "Being" needs, you may recall, are the ones that emerge, according to Maslow, after we have "sufficiently satisfies our "D" or more basic needs for "safety, belongingness, love, respect, and self-esteem." The "B" needs move us to fully utilize our "potentials, capacities, and talents," and to serve some cause beyond that of taking care of ourselves.

The more I thought about the three ways of living with disillusionment described by James, the more clear it became that they were not for me, at least not then. I didn't want to settle for one of them without first exploring the other option he'd suggested.

I was mired in my "why bother" mindset because I'd lost faith in our collective ability to win the battle to shift to a sustainable way of life quickly enough to avert or soften the blow of an eco-crash. There were two ways to get unstuck. One was to rekindle faith in the power of our common sense and our big guns, Science and Technology. The second was to find a way to believe in the existence of an unseen order that was home to some other-than-human powers that might be willing to lend us a hand.

I decided to take on the second task. It would be hard to get my inner skeptic to take on the idea, even as a working hypothesis, that there was room in the natural world for something like James's unseen order. But given how angry I was with Homo Sap. for trashing the planet, it seemed the easier of the two tasks.

There was no way to be sure that James's diagnosis was the correct one for me. But it felt right. Perhaps the best reason to think so was that my mood had lightened after I made the decision to investigate it. I felt I now knew what ailed me and what I had to do to fix it.

What I didn't know was that my attempt to create a picture of an unseen order that I could buy would also lead, unexpectedly, to a reconciliation with my kind.

A note

Thus far I've ignored what James says is another possible cause of his "religious disease." James suggests that the need to believe in his "hidden order" is deeply entrenched in the human psyche. It's always been there and continues to sit there despite all the efforts of the modern mind to root it out. Unrequited, this yearning can create a measure of ongoing angst even for those who do have a strong faith in the power for good of our kind.

But I wasn't persuaded that the yearning was either universal or basic, that is, not born of other things such as the sense of the precariousness of existence or the wish for an afterlife. As such I didn't think it needed to be looked at by itself, independently of our other needs.

4
The end of a phase

The decision to accept James's diagnosis, at least provisionally, marked the end of what I thought of as my time in "the pit." I'd spent fifteen months in it, the last nine in my querencia. I now felt well enough to come out of that hiding place.

I told my colleagues that I was putting my book project on ice. I didn't elaborate. I knew I hadn't quit on my wish to write about our methods, but for now that project had served its purpose. It had given me the vehicle I needed to diagnose what ailed me, and I was eager to get on with the task of putting together a cure.*

I wasn't fully recovered from my angst. If your leg has been in a cast for months it takes a while, after it comes off, for the muscles to regain their strength. But I could walk freely again, even jog a bit.

My mood had begun to lighten after my work with Maslow and Frankl. It feels good to have a handle on your problem, to be assured it's a good one to have, and to see that you have company. Taking on James's diagnosis gave it another big lift. Why?

If you recall, what made it hard for me to get going with the task of aligning my life with my "B" values and aspirations was the feeling that there was nothing I or

* I did eventually write that book, albeit oriented more toward issues encountered at work than outside it. The title: *Managing the People Side of Innovation.*[1]

anyone else could do to avert or soften the blow of the ecological disasters for which we were headed. But perhaps the situation was not as hopeless as I had imagined it was.

Being an agnostic rather than a hard-line disbeliever was of course a prerequisite to being open to the idea that there might be an "unseen order" that included forces that could help us avert or soften the impact of an eco-crash. But the decision to experiment with that idea changed the way I thought about the possibility. The question of whether or not such an order really existed had always felt academic, not one whose answer might have practical implications for me. And so I had not given much thought to what the nature of such Beings or Forces might be. If they existed, could they be ones we could enlist in the fight that mattered to me?

The idea of exploring that possibility appealed to me. If it had any substance it meant there was a chance we could win the fight. But the skeptic in me was not ready to concede that the notion was anything more than an airy speculation. Nevertheless the thought cheered me, kindled a small ember of hope. It gave me the added lift I needed to leave my querencia and get on with the task of aligning my life with my "B" values and aspirations.

This task had, you may remember, three parts:

- Become involved in activities that serve the needs of someone or something other than myself.
- Live in a way that is socially and environmentally responsible.
- Work on my state of mind because the more free it was of inner conflicts and tensions the more effective I was likely to be in doing the first two things.

I now had to include in this list one other thing:

- Create a picture — one I could buy — of a hidden order that included one or more Powers that we could plug into.

The first three of these were clearly things I would have to work on for the rest of my life. The fourth has also turned out that way — I'm still waiting for the moment when some event or insight will in one stroke wipe out all remaining doubts and transform me into a pure believer. But I did manage, over the next few years, to dispel enough of my doubts about whether such Powers could exist to be able to live my life as if they did.

Finding reasons to believe in the existence of any other-than-human power was only the first step in what I needed to do to create an antidote for my angst. I also had to find a conception of specific manifestations of it that could and might want to give us a hand in our fight to save our habitat. And I had to imagine how people involved in that fight could get that assistance without having to accept or even think about the possibility that those powers might exist.

What follows is an account of the ideas and experiences that helped me to do these things.

Part II
Finding a way forward

5

Creating a live hypothesis

> There is no real division between mind and matter, psyche and soma ... before the advent of the quantum theory, our knowledge of matter as gained from the study of physics would have led us to deny that it could have a mental pole ... To pursue this approach further might perhaps extend our knowledge of both poles into new domains.
>
> — David Bohm and B.J. Hiley, *The Undivided Universe* [1]

"Let us give the name of *hypothesis*," says James, "to anything that may be proposed to our belief; and just as the electricians speak of live and dead wires, let us speak of any hypothesis as either live or dead. A live hypothesis is one which appeals as a real possibility to [the person] to whom it is proposed."[2] The same proposition can feel live to one person, dead to another.

My task now was to create a picture — one I could buy — of "an unseen order" in which I could find answers for the "riddles of the [everyday] world," answers that would help me make my peace with it. I didn't work on it in any organized way. I continued to operate as I had in the querencia, doing a lot of reading but basing my choices of what to read more on whim than on logic. And with this task too I might have made quicker progress if I had given more thought to the process, to how I might go about it.

What follows is an account of what I did, arranged in the order in which, after the fact, I wish I had done it.

James had warned me that the hard part of the task, for someone like me, was not going to be finding appealing conceptions of someone or something bigger than Homo Sap., but in squaring them with the part of me that felt "a sort of intellectual loyalty [to] hard facts," for whom "the entity called 'science' was an idol."

I didn't think there was room for any invisible intelligences in science's picture of reality. I'd worked with a lot of scientists and engineers. Some were believers in one or another kind of God, but none of them would have claimed that there were any "hard facts" to support their belief. Those two things — their science and their faith — existed in two separate worlds.

So why couldn't I settle for that arrangement? Because I'd come across some articles and books that claimed that the new physics and recent findings in other areas had produced a conception of the universe that was remarkably similar to that described by Eastern mystics. The books had titles such as *The Tao of Physics*[3] and *The Holographic Paradigm*.[4]

In the introduction to *The Holographic Paradigm* the book's editor, Ken Wilber, says it is a collection of essays extracted from "an extraordinary dialogue [that] occurred in the pages of *ReVision Journal*." The dialogue was about the interface of science and religion. It's one, Wilber notes, that "goes back a long way — at least to Plato, Aristotle and Plotinus (although 'science' didn't mean quite the same thing then as it does now)." But historically

> the discussions usually centered on the differences between science and religion, their conflicts, their competing and apparently irreconcilable truth-claims

> [with an occasional proposal for a] possible armistice [or] some sort of peaceful, if edgy, coexistence.
>
> But here, rather suddenly, in the 1970s, were some very sober, very skilled researchers — physicists, biologists, physiologists, neurosurgeons — and these scientists were not talking *with* religion, they were simply *talking religion*, and more extraordinarily, they were doing so in an attempt to explain the hard data of science itself. The very facts of science, they were saying, [seemed] to make sense only if we assume [some] implicit or unifying or transcendental ground underlying the explicit data.

So perhaps it was possible to create a picture of the world in which both the seeker and the scientist in me could live together.

A hologram, you may recall, is a way of taking a picture of an object without a camera or lens, using coherent radiation such as the light produced by a laser. The "negative" on which the picture is captured looks nothing like the original but when illuminated the right way will project a 3-D image of the object. The negative differs from its conventional counterpart in that every part of it contains information about the entire object. If you cut off a small piece of the negative and illuminate it you still see the whole oak tree (or whatever), though with diminished resolution.

Much of the discussion in *The Holographic Paradigm* was sparked by the work and ideas of Karl Pribram, a neurosurgeon, and the physicist David Bohm. As Wilber notes in his introduction, "Pribram's studies in brain memory and functioning led him to the conclusion that the brain operates, in many ways, like a hologram … The key point [is] that the *part* has access to the *whole*."

And, if the brain does "function like a hologram, then it might have access to a larger whole, a field domain or "holistic frequency realm' that transcended spatial and temporal boundaries. [This] domain, reasoned Pribram, might very likely be the same domain [of] unity-in-diversity described [by] mystics and sages."

Soon after he began to think this way, Pribram became aware of the ideas of the physicist David Bohm, whose "work in subatomic physics [had] led him to the conclusion that physical entities which seemed to be separate and discrete in space and time were actually linked [in] an implicit or underlying fashion. [In] other words, the physical universe itself seemed to be [a projection of] a gigantic hologram." Each part of it has access, through this underlying order, to the whole. And the whole is reflected at some level in each part.

It was primarily the ideas of these two scientists that suggested the term "holographic paradigm." But the underlying notion — that the world of science and that of the mystics may have something in common — had been around for a while. "[Ever] since the "quantum revolution' [various] physicists have been finding intriguing parallels between their results and [the mystics description of the world]. Heisenberg, Bohr, Schroedinger, Eddington, Jeans [and] Einstein all held a mystical-spiritual view of the world." Now, beginning with the 1970s, a lot of people were writing books and articles about these parallels.

I read a lot of these publications, as well as more technical books about the new physics, including several by Bohm. I learned something about quantum mechanics and the theory of relativity but had trouble finding what I was looking for: permission from the world of science to believe that the universe was not merely a mindless, mechanical thing. Two things got in the way.

One was lack of clarity about what constituted the permission that I sought. The other was that the connections people made between the two worlds seemed tenuous. Worse, there was something about the way the links were made that troubled me, an unease I couldn't ascribe to anything specific.

Eventually I got through these difficulties with the help of another book Wilber assembled as a kind of sequel to *The Holographic Paradigm*. Called *Quantum Questions*,[5] its core is a collection of essays by eight of the founders of the new physics (Max Planck, James Jeans, Albert Einstein, Arthur Eddington, Erwin Schroedinger, Louis de Broglie, Wolfgang Pauli, and Werner Heisenberg.)

Wilber helped me see how to get to what I needed from the world of science, and for this I owe him thanks. But it wasn't easy for me to let him help because there were things he said in these two books that didn't sound right to me. Such as the fact that all eight of the physicists in his collection were mystics. Seemed an overly loose use of the word. I also had trouble with his assertion that the worldview of all acknowledged mystics is rigidly hierarchical. Didn't jibe with what felt to me like the more authentic description of it in Aldous Huxley's book, *The Perennial Philosophy*.

These kinds of misgivings about some of Wilber's ideas made it hard to see others he had that were both valid and helpful. Perhaps because I feel indebted to him I focus, in what follows, more on the ideas I found useful than the ones I couldn't swallow.

Here's what I learned from him.

Be aware of the pitfalls

Perhaps because I wanted to find an "unseen order" in the new physics I ignored the warning Wilber gave, in *The Holographic Paradigm*, to anyone who sets off on that venture. Perhaps also because he buried the warning in the middle of the book. But he posted it up front in the sequel, *Quantum Questions*. It helped me understand what it was that had bothered me about the attempt to link the "hard facts" of science to the mystic's world of spirit.

"In the past decade," Wilber says in his introduction to *Quantum Questions*, "There have [appeared] dozens of books [purporting] to describe or explain [the] relationship between modern physics, the hardest science, and mysticism, the tenderest of religions."

"[It is] tempting and appealing," he adds, "to be able to claim that physics — the "really real' science — actually supports mysticism. I, in my [earlier] writings, did exactly that. But it [was a mistake]."

Why? Because building a case — say for the existence of a Universal Intelligence — on what quantum mechanics has discovered about the world of subatomic particles can backfire in one or all of three ways.

The big danger

The first problem is that you are trying to build a stable belief system on ideas that may be on the center stage of physics today but may not be there tomorrow. One author, Wilber notes, "put much stake in bootstrap theory (which says there are no irreducible things, only self-consistent relationships) and equated this with the Buddhist mystical doctrine of mutual interpenetration. But nowadays virtually all physicists believe there are irreducible things (quarks, leptons, gluons) that arise out of broken symmetries. Does Buddha therefore lose his enlightenment?"

Every one of the physicists Wilber quotes in *Quantum Questions* was alert to this danger. They were aware that their new science was like a child prodigy, capable of remarkable feats (like paving the way to nuclear power), but not done growing up.

Quantum theory's mathematical descriptions of subatomic reality did a great job of predicting behavior in that world. But it lacked a solid bridge to classical physics (the one we rely on to deal with our everyday "macro" world). It also hadn't yet figured out how to hook up with the other half of the new physics, the theory of relativity. And its math said some things that sounded nonsensical —such as that maybe whether an electron behaves like a particle or an energy wave depends solely on the way humans choose to look at it. Filling in these and other gaps in their theory would likely require them to modify or even discard some of its elements. And so these scientists were careful to hedge any statements they made about what their findings might imply about the nature of things in general.

"The philosophic trend of modern scientific thought differs markedly from the views of thirty years ago," said Eddington back in 1927. "Can we guarantee that the next thirty years will not see another revolution, perhaps even a complete reaction?"

And so, he says, "[This] lack of finality of scientific theories would be a serious limitation of [any speculations] that staked much on their permanence. The religious reader may well be content that I have not offered [a] God revealed by quantum theory, and therefore likely to be swept away in the next scientific revolution."[6]

Two generations later the final picture of the quantum world is still evolving and, according to some physicists, we may never get to see all of it.

Of the three dangers Wilber brought to my attention this was the one I felt I needed to look out for the most. I was looking for a "go" sign in science, and when you have an acute need to find something you are likely to see things that aren't really there. I was less concerned about his other two warnings.

The second pitfall

It is tempting, Wilber says, to think that there is a shortcut to enlightenment. There are many who "[encourage] the belief that [to] achieve mystical awareness all one need do is learn a new worldview; since physics and mysticism are simply two different approaches to the same reality, why bother with years of arduous meditation? Just read *The Tao of Physics*." To be fair to Capra, who wrote that book, he adds that you can take away this message from such books even when that's not what the author wants you to do.

I wasn't worried about falling into this trap. I was not looking for satori, my aim was not to merge my consciousness with that of some Universal Intelligence. Perhaps I would experience that someday, but for now all I wanted to do was to make the idea that such Beings could exist seem plausible to me. And two, even in this more modest context I was wary of psychic get-rich-quick schemes. I didn't think there was any easy path to inner peace, whether through belief in an unseen order or in any other way, perhaps not even for James's sunny people who needed to be born only once.

If anything, I felt I needed to guard against the opposite tendency — to discount progress that seemed to have been made too easily. It can be that you've already done a lot of work on a problem, though you may not be aware of all you've done. In such cases coming across one idea phrased right may be all it takes to break up a logjam in the psyche.

The third kind of danger

People who venture on this path, warns Wilber, are susceptible to the sin of "reductionist" thinking. Making the leap, for example, from "atoms in the brain play a part in the thought process" to "therefore the mind is nothing more than a collection of atoms."

He quotes one writer who "thinks absolute spirit is a photon," and another who claims to have demonstrated that God is an electron. The first statement, he says, was made by the head of an institute that studies consciousness, the second by a French physicist. He doesn't think either one was joking.

It seemed to me that in thinking about the nature of an Ultimate Being much of the confusion arises from a failure to keep something in mind: that it can be both immanent and transcendent. God, if there is one, can permeate everything and can at the same time be beyond all things. You may be able to feel the presence of God even in a tiny particle if you meditate on it in the right way. That doesn't mean God is the sum of all such particles in the universe.

Perhaps there are other reasons why people fall into this kind of "reductionist" thinking trap. But I didn't think it was one that was likely to snare me, once I'd been made aware of it. I could thank Wilber for that and move on.

Be clear about what constitutes permission

Quantum Questions, you may recall, is a collection of essays by eight of the physicists who helped create the new physics (Planck, Jeans, Einstein, Eddington, Schroedinger, de Broglie, Pauli, Heisenberg). In his preface to the book, Wilber claims that they all say, in essence, "that modern physics offers no positive support (let alone proof) for a mystical worldview." But, he assures me, this didn't mean that I could find no help in it to make that worldview seem more plausible to me. How come?

Because, Wilber says, despite their insistence that there was no basis for it in the new physics, "every one of [them] was a mystic." So, "If they did not get their mysticism from a study of modern physics, where did they get it? And why?" It was in the answers to these questions, he suggested, that I would find the help I sought.

I read his collection of their writings. I also read several of the books from which they were extracted. Were they all mystics? Yes, if they can be called that because they believed in an unseen order and were open to the idea of an Order Maker. No, if you take the word to mean someone who claims to have made contact with a Maker. Yes again if it is sufficient to have apprehended directly, intuitively, at least some of the material aspects of that order.

Did they all unequivocally say that there was nothing in the world revealed by the new physics that supported their mystical views? Yes and no. Each of them did publicly say this. But many also said things that seemed to contradict this assertion. Here's James Jeans on both sides of the fence.

He says, in one essay:

> What of the things which are not seen which religion assures us are eternal? There has been much discussion of late of the claims of [scientific support for transcendental events]. Speaking as a scientist, I find the alleged proofs totally unconvincing; speaking as a human being, I find most of them ridiculous as well. [7]

But elsewhere he also says:

> Today there is a wide measure of agreement, which on the physical side of science approaches almost to unanimity, that the stream of knowledge is heading towards a non-mechanical reality; the universe begins to look more like a great thought than like a great machine. Mind no longer appears as an accidental intruder into the realm of matter; we are beginning to suspect that we ought rather to hail it as the creator and governor of the realm of matter — not of course our individual minds, but the mind in which the atoms out of which our individual minds have grown exist as thoughts.[8]

He also says this mind may be that "of some Eternal Spirit."

Why is there this "wide measure of agreement" among his peers? Because the hard data from their experiments can confirm only mathematical descriptions of the subatomic world, not its ultimate nature. All they can be sure of is the existence of mathematical laws that are part of that nature.

If that's as far as the data can go, it of course can't say anything about whether or not there is some kind of Universal Mind out there. What it can do is to open a door, in the minds of Jeans and his peers, that allows their highly developed intuitive powers to investigate that possibility.

Wilber, in answering the question about why these eight physicists held views he calls "mystical," makes no use of anything they say that appears to contradict their assertion that their science provides no support for mysticism. He ignores it in part because it violates his first injunction: do not look for such support in what science says about the nature of the world, because what it says is subject to change. But he also ignores it because of another bias he brings to the endeavor.

This bias arises from his take on the worldview of the mystics. He sees it as a tightly furled hierarchy. It's a variation of the old idea of the "great chain of being": Matter at the bottom. Then, in order, life, mind, and in Wilber's picture, three kinds of levels of spirit. It's a strictly one-way scheme in which higher levels encompass lower ones and can therefore inform them in nontrivial ways, but not the other way around. So the world of physics, which deals with the lowest level of matter, can, by definition, never ever reveal anything significant about the levels above it, especially those furthest removed from it.

But these scientists, Wilber knows, are very familiar with the literature on the subject. They are also well aware of the danger in building a case for mysticism on shifting ground. But every now and then they say things that seem to violate one or both of his injunctions. Why?

At first I was mildly irritated by Wilber's failure to follow these trails. Paradoxes can be illuminating. But eventually I was thankful that he ignored them. By adhering strictly to his rules of admissible evidence he found support for the mystic view in modern physics that was based not on any of its specific findings but in the nature of its inquiry. It was a case that felt solid to my inner skeptic. The "argument for" smelled clean, no whiff in it of the thinking errors he didn't want to make. Here is the gist of that argument.

What Wilber hears these scientists say is, in essence, that Plato was right. As Eddington put it:

> We have learnt that the exploration of the external world by the methods of physical science leads not to a concrete reality but to a *shadow world of symbols*, beneath which those methods are unadapted for penetrating.[9]

And what, Wilber asks, "did the new physics [tell them] that the old physics failed to mention?" About that, he says, there is "a general and common conclusion reached by the majority of the theorists in this volume."

This conclusion "is best elucidated by Schroedinger and Eddington." The great difference between the old and the new physics, Wilber hears them saying, "is not that the latter is relativistic, non-deterministic, four-dimensional, or any of those sorts of things. The great difference [is] both much simpler and much more profound: both the old and the new physics were dealing with shadow symbols, but the new physics was forced to be aware of that fact — forced to be aware that it was dealing with shadows [and] not reality."

Schroedinger puts it this way:

> Please note that [it is not the recent advances in physics that have given its world] this shadowy character; it had [been there] ever since Democritus of

Abdera and even before, but we were not aware of it; we thought we were dealing with the world itself.[10]

And James Jeans says:

> The essential fact is simply that all the pictures which science now draws of nature, and which alone seem capable of according with observational fact, are mathematical pictures … They are nothing more than [that] — fictions if you like, if by fiction you mean that [they are not based on any] ultimate reality. Many would hold that [the] outstanding achievement of twentieth-century physics is not the theory of relativity with its welding together of space and time, or the theory of quanta with its apparent negation of the laws of causation, or the dissection of the atom with the resultant discovery that things are not what they seem; it is the general recognition that we are not yet in contact with ultimate reality. We are still imprisoned in our cave, with our backs to the light, and can only watch the shadows on the wall.[11]

If you think that the world of your science is in essence that of Plato's cave, you grant that there is another world outside it, and that is where the source is of the light that casts the shadows. And that even if the tools of your science can tell you nothing about its nature, it cannot rule out the possibility that it is out there. Here are some things Eddington says after finding himself in this situation.

> [If] you want to fill a vessel with something you must make it hollow, and the old-fashioned material body was not hollow enough to be a receptacle of mental or of spiritual attributes. The result was to place consciousness in the position of an intruder in the physical world …
>
> Our present conception [of it] is hollow enough to hold almost anything. [What] we are dragging to light as the basis of all phenomena is a scheme of

> symbols connected by mathematical equations. That is what physical reality boils down to when probed by the methods which a physicist can apply. A skeleton scheme of symbols proclaims its own hollowness. It can be — nay it cries out to be — filled with something that shall transform it from skeleton into substance, [from] symbols into an interpretation of the symbols."

And how does this change his stance, as a scientist, toward an unseen order?

> The bearing of physical science on religion is that the scientist has from time to time assumed the duty of signalman and set up warnings of danger — not always unwisely. If I interpret the present situation rightly, a main-line signal which had been standing at danger has now been lowered. But nothing much is going to happen unless there is an engine.[12]

That engine, he implies, has to be our desire to travel on that line and see where it takes us. What are we likely to find on our journey?

> We have seen that [the] scheme of physics presupposes a background outside the scope of its investigations. In this background we must find, first, our own personality, and then perhaps a greater personality. The idea of a Universal Mind or Logos would be, I think, a fairly plausible inference from the present state of scientific theory; at least it is in harmony with it. But if so, all that our inquiry justifies us in asserting is a purely colorless pantheon. Science cannot tell whether the world-spirit is good or evil, and its halting argument for the existence of a God might equally be turned into an argument for the existence of a Devil.

Is there really anything to be found out there? Science can offer no guarantee of that. The only way to find out may be to go on that journey, so don't waste a lot of time trying to figure it out beforehand.

> We are anxious for perfect truth, but it is hard to say in what form [it] is to be found. [Physicists are] not conscious of any disloyalty to truth on occasions when [their] sense of proportion tells [them] to regard a plank as continuous material, well knowing that it is "really' empty space containing sparsely scattered electric charges.
>
> [So here] I am standing on the threshold about to enter a room. It is a complicated business... I must make sure of landing on a plank traveling at twenty miles a second round the sun — a fraction of a second too early or too late, the plank would be miles away. I must do this whilst hanging from a round planet head outward into space, and with a wind of aether blowing at no one knows how many miles a second through every interstice of my body. The plank has no solidity of substance. To step on it is like stepping on a swarm of flies. Shall I not slip through? [These] are really minor difficulties. I ought really to look at the problem four-dimensionally as concerning the intersection of my world-line with that of the plank. Then again it is necessary to determine in which direction the entropy of the world is increasing in order to be sure that my passage over the threshold is an entrance, not an exit.
>
> Verily it is easier for a camel to pass through the eye of a needle than for a [scientist] to pass through a door. And whether [it] be a barn [or] church door it might be wiser [to] consent to be an ordinary [person] and walk in rather than wait until all the difficulties involved in a really scientific egress are resolved.[13]

What Wilber and these physicists helped me do was to move the idea of an unseen order across the threshold on something like the following scale of plausibility:

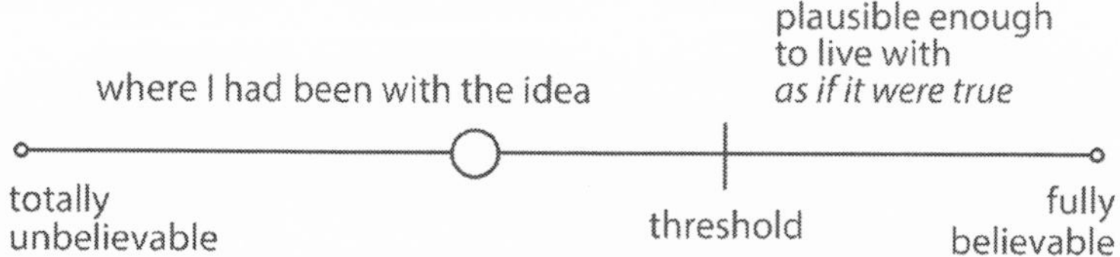

Given the nature of the part of me that needed to feel the hypothesis was a "live" one, permission to move it past the threshold had to come from the world of science. It would have been hard for me to find people I thought were more qualified to speak for it than these eight scientists.

Getting this permission was only part of my task. The other was to decide what kinds of powers I wanted to put in my picture of the unseen order. I'd been going back and forth between the two parts. In retrospect I wish I had focused on the first thing first because until I was done with it my inner skeptic generated so much noise that it was hard to think clearly about the second part. The skeptic was still around, but a lot more open-minded than before. And not as loud.

6
Things to keep in mind

> A moral question is a question not of what sensibly exists, but of what is good, or would be good if it did exist.
>
> — William James[1]

After I got the permission I needed to go ahead and develop my idea of an unseen order, I recalled some things William James had said that helped me to do this work. Here, in essence, is what he told me to keep in mind. (The quotes in what follows are all from *The Varieties of Religious Experience.*)

Be clear about where you are going

I needed to be reminded that James had helped me make my peace with a word that could be used to describe where I was headed — toward "religion." The word had unpleasant associations for me. I wanted to have nothing to do with any institutionalized version of it. My spirit felt stifled by any kind of doctrinal thinking. And it was not hard to find accounts of the horrors committed by religious fanatics, unchecked if not abetted or instigated by their leaders. I'd not only read about them but, as a child, had lived through the nastiness that accompanied the partition of India and seen how religion could foster murderous madness.

James made it clear that my personal unseen order need have nothing to do with any formal creed or dogma. There is, he says, a "great partition which divides the religious field. On the one side of it lies institutional, on the other personal religion. [Procedures and] theology and ceremony and ecclesiastical organization are the essentials [in] the institutional branch ... In the more personal branch [it] is on the contrary the inner dispositions of [individuals themselves] which form the center of interest."

Theology may play a part in it, but "the acts [which the second] sort of religion prompts are personal not ritual acts. [You transact] the business by [yourself] alone, and the ecclesiastical organization, with its priests and sacraments and other go-betweens, sinks to an altogether secondary place. The relation goes direct from heart to heart, from soul to soul, between [you and your] maker." You could, he adds, give this personal religion some other name. "Call it conscience or morality, if [you] prefer." In the context of his book, he says:

> Religion [shall] mean for us *the feelings, acts, and experiences of [individuals] in their solitude, so far as they apprehend themselves to stand in relation to whatever they may consider the divine.*

This way of defining the word worked for me as well. Getting clear about where I was headed helped reassure me that I wouldn't catch any of the contagions I associated with organized religion.

OK, so I'd gotten my psychic flu-shot, but I was also walking into a place where there was a profusion of ideas about the nature of "the divine." There were those of the monists, the polytheists, the naturalists, the supernaturalists, the mystics, and any number of others. Without some more help from James I could have got lost in all those idea thickets. He suggested I use the following guidelines to find my way through them.

Go for a personal relationship

Does the "divine" element in either kind of religion have to be a being? It's not a requirement, says James.

> There are systems of thought which [are called] religions, and yet which do not positively assume a God. Buddhism is in this case. Popularly, of course, the Buddha himself stands in place of a God, but in strictness the Buddhistic system is atheistic. Modern transcendental idealism, Emersonianism, for instance, also seems to let God evaporate into abstract Ideality. Not a deity *in concreto*, not a superhuman person, but the immanent divinity in things, the essentially spiritual structure of the universe.

In the Emersonian kind of religion,

> The universe has a divine soul of order, which soul is moral, being also the soul within [us]. But whether this soul of the universe be a mere quality like the eye's brilliancy or the skin's softness, or whether it be a self-conscious life like the eye's seeing or the skin's feeling, is a decision that never appears in Emerson's pages. It quivers on the boundary of these things, sometimes leaning one way, sometimes the other, to suit the literary rather than the philosophic need. Whatever it is, though, it is active. As much as if it were a God, we can trust it to protect all ideal interests and keep the world's balance straight.

If abstract Ideality is at one end of the spectrum of conceptions of the divine, then at the other end are one or more Beings with whom we can establish a personal relationship. The more abstract end was easier to sell to my inner skeptic, but James convinced me to move, along with him, to the other end. What I found persuasive was that he went there for pragmatic reasons.

"[Some] schools of philosophy," he says, "have too often overlooked the fact that [our] thinking is organically connected with [our] conduct." And so we need to ask, about whatever we choose to believe in, how does that faith inform the way we live our lives? What does it do for us or for our world? What, in this sense, is its "cash value"?

What I heard James say, in effect, was that I could stick to the abstract end if that worked for me, but I was likely to find more sustenance for my spirit at the other end -- if I was able to find a concept there that I could live with.

Establishing a one-to-one relationship with the divine, he says, opens a channel for an "actual inflow of energy." The interaction may be with an imaginary being, but the energy gain is real, as are the changes it facilitates in the way you think and feel about things. It kindles hope for the causes you care about. And it makes you feel more aligned with some purpose larger than any of yours.

Moving to the "being" end of the spectrum doesn't mean you have to let go of the notion that certain moral laws may be part of the nature of the universe, as impersonal as Newton's laws of motion. Only that you are open to the possibility that there may be a Law Maker.

And if you don't succeed in finding a plausible concept of a Being with whom you can get connected, you still have the option to go live with Emerson.

Remember, this picture is for you, not the theologians

When you create your conception of an unseen order, how much attention should you pay to what theologians and philosophers say about its nature? Not much, says James, unless they are pragmatists who believe "that the best method of discussing points of theory is to begin by [asking] what practical difference would result from one alternative or the other being true."

Theologians love to speculate about God's characteristics and have endless debates about them. But, he asks, to what end?

> Take [arguments for] God's aseity,* for example, [or] immateriality [or] "simplicity' [or] self-sufficiency [or whatever] — candidly speaking, how do such qualities [make] any definite connection with our life?
>
> [Now], what specific act can I perform in order to adapt myself the better to God's simplicity? Or how does it assist me to plan my behavior, to know that [God's] happiness [is] absolutely complete?

James goes on to talk about other "points of theory" that he feels free to ignore. These include:

The argument that the law of causality is violated by the notion of a Being that can influence the course of events.

> For [some] the world of the ideal has no efficient causality, and never bursts into the world of phenomena at particular points ... It cannot get down upon the flat level of experience and interpolate itself piecemeal between distinct portions of [nature].
>
> I suppose my belief that in communion with the Ideal new force comes into the world, and new departures are made here below, [makes me a supernaturalist] of [the] crasser type. [In any other] way of taking the ideal world, the essence of practical religion evaporates. Both instinctively and for logical reasons, I find it hard to believe that principles exist which make no difference in facts.

Doesn't sit well with the pragmatist in him. Why bother putting together a conception of the divine — whether a set of principles or a Being — if you believe neither can make anything happen in the real world?

---

* aseity: existence originating from and having no source other than itself.

Yes, he notes, it can be said that "we owe it to the Absolute that we have a world of fact at all." But for him, "all facts are particular facts," things that exist in our everyday world. And so his interest in the question of God's existence lies "in the consequences for particulars which that existence may [have]."

Arguments in which God is "assumed as a matter of course to be 'one and only' and to be 'infinite.'"

Hardly anyone, James says, "thinks it worthwhile to consider, and still less to uphold" the notion of "many finite gods." But, he asks, why not?

> I feel bound to say that religious experience [cannot] be cited as unequivocally supporting the infinitist belief. The only thing that it unequivocally testifies to is that we experience union with *something* larger than ourselves and in that union we find our greatest peace.

Those with a "passion for unity" or a "monoideistic bent" are free to identify that something "with a unique God who is the all-inclusive soul of the world."

But, he says, "the practical needs and experiences of religion seem to me sufficiently met" by the belief in some power that is "both other and larger than our conscious selves." And that is friendly to us and our ideals. "Anything larger will do … It need not be infinite, it need not be solitary."

And if this opens a door that lets "a sort of polytheism return upon us," so be it. James makes a philosophical case for why this may not be a bad thing. I think he would not have had any problem with my take on it: So what, if it enables you to align your life with your highest values and aspirations.

James's advice made sense to me. And so in what follows the development of my concept of an unseen order was guided not by any theological considerations but my own inclusion criteria. To become part of my unseen order an idea needs to be one I find both appealing and plausible. To satisfy the second condition it has to meet three requirements:

- It doesn't violate any of the laws of physics or chemistry or biology that I know about.
- In the case of a principle or entity, I can imagine how it could have arisen and might operate — explanations that seem reasonable to me, even if they exist only in my head.
- It is consistent with my experiences and intuitions.

I talk next about the ideas and experiences that helped me find these candidates for inclusion, but I don't say which became part of my unseen order until the second to last chapter. Why? For two reasons.

One is that my search for that order took me to a place from which I could see a way of doing something about our eco-crisis that not only felt promising but was one in which participation did not require belief in any such unseen order. To underscore this point a sketch of that way forward is provided first.

The second reason is this. You may also wish to create a picture of an unseen order that you can buy. But the details of your picture may need to differ from the ones I put in mine. You may have different inclusion criteria. You may want to let the idea of a Universal Intelligence "evaporate into abstract ideality" to a greater or lesser degree than I did. Knowing which candidate ideas became part of my unseen order may make it harder to hear what your intuition and feelings say about whether or not they belong in your picture of it.

The concept of an unseen order that I developed for myself is not a fixed one. Some parts of it stayed put over time, but not others. It will likely never stop evolving. By the time you read this, it may have become different from the one I describe here later.

7

Selecting your sources

By their fruits ye shall know them.

— Matthew, 7:20

Put into words what remains to be done

It took several months of reading and scribbling to do what I describe in the last two chapters: to get, from the world of science, assurance that nothing in it ruled out the possible existence of the unseen order I sought; and from James, clarity about where I was headed. What I needed to do next was to start filling in my picture of that order. But instead of getting on with that task I decided to take a break from it. At least that's what I thought I was doing.

Recall that by now I had emerged from my querencia. I continued to work on my personal problem but gave it less time as I got on with other things. One of these was a wish that preceded my funk: to do more work with Native American groups. I'd run a session for some Cherokee in North Carolina before I disappeared into my "book" project. Now I began to look for ways to do more such work.

Turned out to be what I needed to do to move forward with my task. But because I didn't see that the two things were related my progress was slow. Could it have been quicker? Perhaps if I had taken some time to get clear about what remained to be done. I knew from my work that it helped to phrase these tasks as goals that are specific enough so it's easy to see whether you've accomplished them. In my case they were to:

- Make feel more solid the idea that there are powers or principles out there that can, if appropriate, respond to an individual creature's needs.
- Get some ideas about what we — as individuals and collectively — could do to make it more likely that these "invisibles" would help us avoid or minimize the impact of an eco-crash.
- Find work that would help restore the sense that my life had a purpose and meaning. I once had that feeling and had lost it.

These were not three independent goals. The last was an end I could attain only if I was able to do the first two things.

Look for belief systems with a matching "bottom line"

There was no need for me to create my conception of an unseen order in the sense of dreaming up the elements I wanted to put in it. These are things people have thought about ever since they began to think. Every culture and school of philosophy has its variations on the theme. But where to begin to look for the ideas that are likely to work for you?

I stumbled into an answer to this question that was right for me. It was to look at the traditional Native American view of reality. But I could have got to the answer in a less roundabout way if I'd followed James's advice.

Look, he had said, at how any given belief system informs the way people live their lives. What does it do for them and their world? I wouldn't have had to think hard about this for the answer to become clear. Given the nature of my angst it made sense for me to look at the Native American conception of the natural world and our place in it. It had helped them to live sustainably without trashing their ecosystem.

Native Americans aren't the only ones whose belief systems contain elements that promote a sustainable way of life. I happened to be drawn to their world. And it felt accessible, perhaps because I lived where they did.

The more inspired we feel by the example of how some people live, the more likely we are to find in their constructs of reality the ideas that sustain our spirits. Look into the Native American experience if it moves you, but look also at that of others. You may, for example, find inspiration in the way one or more of the following live (or lived) their lives: the Amish, Australian Aboriginals, Bahais, Essenes, Sufis, Shakers, Tibetan Buddhists, Transcendentalists, Unitarians, or Vedantists. Or any of the others we could add to this list.

In your search you may want to keep one other thing in mind. My experience in helping people to find fresh ideas for a wide variety of problems suggests that they are most likely to be found in places that feel a bit alien and unsettling. These are indicators that you've come across ideas that rattle some of your existing assumptions about how things are or ought to be. Shaking free of them is often a precondition for insight.

Clarify what you do and don't need to learn about the source

I got what I needed from Native American conceptions of the world without having to become an expert about their history or languages or creation myths. And the time I've spent in or near their traditional world has, thus far, been brief. I found I needed to learn only enough to feel that my ideas about them were not inconsistent with those of at least some experts. Beyond that I had to rely primarily on my sense of whether a person or idea I encountered was to be trusted.

In what follows I talk about the help I received from the "traditional Native American" world. But is there or was there ever such a thing?

By some estimates there were, pre-Columbus, perhaps as many as two thousand separate cultures in North America. Many spoke "mutually unintelligible languages ... eighty [in] the Pacific Northwest alone."[1] And so I had to be careful about what I attributed collectively to such a diverse group of independent peoples.

The thing they did seem to have in common was a relationship with the land that enabled them to live sustainably on it for thousands of years. And some core beliefs about the nature of things that shaped that scheme for living. I've met a few who hold onto that traditional worldview, and I've read what many others of them have said about it. They belong to different tribes, have different names for things, but they all share a certain stance toward the earth.

But were they really great stewards of the land? We're talking about how they lived hundreds of years ago before we upset their scheme for living, whatever it was. And they left no written descriptions of the values and perceptions of the world that shaped that scheme.

Some groups did make glyphic records[2] of major annual events, often referring to themselves in the third person: "They scatter over the plain," "Cold winter, ravens freeze in trees," "They use pipe in new ceremony of affection toward children," "Two from enemy tribe kill their leader." Not enough material for a *Tale of Two Cities* or a history of the Tang Dynasty. To create the Native equivalent of such works these brief snapshots had to be supplemented by their oral "archives."

There are those who think they were a childlike folk without the ambition — or the smarts, or both — to develop the technology needed to build empires and cities and cathedrals or, in time, to invent steel and gunpowder.

I never bought that idea. Perhaps because I got my first impressions of their traditional way of life from books by or about those among them who have held on to their old ways of seeing and thinking about things. The Traditionals are talkers, not writers, so what I read were "as told to" accounts set on paper by non-Natives. But in several of them the Native voice seemed to come through undistorted.[3]

What that voice said to me was that they knew what they were doing. They didn't take the heavy footprint route not because they weren't clever enough to take it, but because doing so was inconsistent with their values. Their cousins in Central and South America did take that route, and there was evidence of at least one experiment in that direction in the U.S. (Cahokia). What about their capacity to develop technology? If the account of their ancestry was correct, their Chinese cousins were the first to make explosives.

I accepted what that voice told me because it felt true. But it nevertheless felt good to learn subsequently of new research findings that discredit the idea that Native Americans were content to play whatever hand nature dealt them, and so made minimal changes to the ecosystems into which they settled. True perhaps in the far North where nature put tight limits on what they could do. But not elsewhere.

The newer findings suggest that they weren't stewards of the land in the sense that they maintained it in its primeval wild state. They were very active portfolio managers. Fire was one of the tools they used to sculpt the landscape. Tribes in the Northeast used it to create a parkland like ecosystem. But it was done in such a way that it looked wild to Europeans. And far to their south studies in the supposedly primeval rain forests have suggested that certain areas are actually plantations, managed by people classed as "gatherers."[4]

So did they deliberately eschew the kind of development that would ultimately prove unsustainable, or were they deficient in their ambitions? Or perhaps held back, as Diamond suggests (in *Guns, Germs and Steel*), by an unfortunate lack of some key natural resources? (I didn't find his thesis convincing.)

For my purposes it wasn't necessary to find definitive answers to these questions. All I needed was to be clear about the part of their story that mattered to me.

They had lived here for a very long time (the old twelve- to fourteen-thousand years estimate keeps getting pushed back). Their numbers didn't exceed the carrying capacity of the land. The air, the waters, and the earth remained unpolluted. What is known about their laws, customs, and conceptions of the cosmos makes it clear that certain ideas shaped the way they related to the earth and to all that lived on it. Enough to make their world feel like the right place for me to go to for what I needed.

In your case, you may need to look to some other source for the ideas you need to create an antidote for your eco-angst. And so the aspects of that culture that you do or don't need to check out may be different.

Take a level stance

When we look to other cultures for help in solving our problems we run two kinds of risks. One arises from the tendency to idealize them. This makes it hard to see which are the things that we can profitably borrow from them and which we should not try to adopt. It also makes us prone to dissing our own culture. Many of my kind of Indians stepped into both these traps with regard to the Brits. Wow, they can make the trains run on time. Let's try to be like them in every way, never mind that in doing so we may lose valuable chunks of our own heritage.

The other kind of risk arises from the opposite tendency, to not fully open ourselves to others' ideas because doing so may imply that we are their inferiors.

I regularly see examples of both tendencies in my work. They make it hard to transfer good ideas and practices from one part of a company to another, or across the borders between different kinds of industries or technologies or academic disciplines.

The most productive kind of cross-fertilization takes place when both sides view each other as intellectual equals with different sets of accomplishments. Even in areas in which one group has experienced success and the other failure, both have something to learn from each other.

I had to remind myself of these things because my initial tendency was to put the Native American world on a pedestal. Yes, you need to approach your chosen teachers respectfully and with a good measure of humility. But without turning them into oracles about everything, including stuff you may know more about than them. The teachers I've admired the most have been those who, despite their achievements, remained open to learning from others, including their students.

What follows after this chapter is an account of how I found, in the Native American world, the ideas I needed to assemble a picture of my unseen order. If you want to look elsewhere for the ideas you need, you may want to keep in mind some of the things that helped me to make my search productive. These are:

Experience the world of your source directly, don't rely only on what others say about it.

The quickest way to discover what anyone else's world can do for you may be to seek its help with a real problem. By real I mean one:

- That matters to you.
- Whose resolution serves a purpose beyond enhancing only your wellbeing(except when you first need to get well to be able to do something for your world).

Take only what you need.

- Keep in mind that you seek to create a picture of an unseen order in which you can find hope of winning the fight against the evils that most trouble you.
- The worldviews in which you look for elements of that picture may include, along with ideas you can use, some that it may be best to leave alone. Either because they are too foreign to your way of thinking, or because they may lead you astray.

The idea I felt I ought to stay away from was that it was possible to acquire "strange powers," a term used for such things as the ability to sense what's going on in another person's mind or body. Or to communicate, mind to mind, at a distance. The latter is an ability considered unusual but normal in many traditional cultures. The Australian Aboriginals would say, "Oh yeah, the bush telephone."

Cultures in which there's little doubt that you can develop such abilities also include a warning: it's OK to do that if it enables you to serve some larger-than-you cause; otherwise you can get drunk with the power and do things that harm others and, ultimately, yourself.

8
A sequence of events

> [There] is the question of what is the relationship of thinking to reality … Does the content of thought merely give us abstract and simplified snapshots of reality, or can it go further, somehow to grasp the very essence of the living moments that we sense in actual experience?
>
> — David Bohm
> *Wholeness and the Implicate Order*[1]

As you may recall, I needed two kinds of help from the Native world. One was to make feel more solid the notion that there is an unseen order that includes powers that can make things happen in the real world. The other was to find ideas that had once enabled Native Americans to live sustainably and that could be transplanted to the modern world.

I got a measure of both kinds of help from a sequence of events related to three healing ceremonies in which I was a participant. Here's how I got to be in them.

Not long after I began to look for ways to work with Native American groups I got a call from someone who had been in one of my workshops.* He thought his brother, Greg, could use our problem-solving methods in his work. Greg's wife, Alice, was Navajo. They lived on the

* Some of the people in this episode did not want me to use their real names, so I've renamed them all.

Reservation in a hogan Greg built on land traditionally assigned to Alice's family. Greg, a non-Native, was trusted enough in the community to have been made the Director of the Tribal Government's Department of Agriculture. I ran several sessions for his team.

I continued to work with him when, after a few years, he quit that job and began working with other Native groups. What he liked to do was to help communities to translate their objectives into practical projects and, if necessary, find money for them. He could do these things more easily when not encumbered by the kind of hurdles to action that seem to thrive in any large organization.

One day I got a call from a cousin. Indira was in London, along with her husband and father. She had been ill for a few years. The treatment she got in India wasn't working. Her doctors there had run out of ideas. They thought what she had left was most likely six to eighteen months of life.

My cousin was a fighter. She decided to get other opinions from specialists outside India, one in London, the other in L.A. Both were very busy men. The earliest the American could see her was a couple of months after the Brit.

She decided to use those months working with some nonconventional American therapists who lived on the East Coast. She wanted to use the Boston area, where I lived, as her base. She knew I was working with some Native groups, and had read *Rolling Thunder*, a book about a traditional Cherokee medicine man. While she was here, could I arrange for her to work with a traditional Native American healer?

I told her the odds of my being able to do that were low. It was not easy for non-Natives to find them. If you did manage to contact them it was unlikely they would agree to work with you if it didn't feel right for them to do so, even if they needed the money you were willing to give them for their services. Any you found who did it for just the money were likely to do you more harm than good. But I would try.

I called Greg. Yes, his wife knew a traditional healer who had conducted several healing ceremonies for members of not only her but also his family. Perhaps she'd be willing to do one for my cousin. For her to say yes to that she'd need to first meet either my cousin or me. "Could happen," Greg said, "But you know how the Traditionals are."

He and his wife had moved from the Res and now lived in Flagstaff. Bella, the medicine woman, lived a five-hour drive away. Where she might be at any time, on or off the Res, was unpredictable. Her movements were guided by something other than our kinds of schedules. "You'd need to come out here and hang out," Greg said. "No telling for how long. And if you do get to meet her, no way to know if she'd want to work with you."

My schedule was also unpredictable. There were a few bits of work that clients wanted me to put in my calendar six or more months ahead of time. But the bulk of it got on the schedule with only a few weeks' notice. After many years of living that way, it didn't feel like an existence that was unduly precarious.

The plus was that there were gaps in my schedule that I could use to hang out in Arizona. They'd need to coincide with times when Greg was in town and not away tending to his projects. Felt doable.

My cousin arrived in Boston, along with her father and husband. I'd found a pleasant apartment for them. I paid for it. Uncle protested but let me do what I wanted. He owned a very profitable business, didn't need any help with the rent. But he was pleased with my gesture, perhaps because he saw I felt it was the right thing for me to do. Mom — his sister — and I lived with him for a couple of years when I was a child. And his current house in Delhi was always open to me. He would have been offended if I stayed anyplace else when I was in town. I lived in a small apartment so they couldn't stay with me. I was glad I'd found a suitable alternative.

But I was not so glad about the business of finding a traditional healer for my cousin if it meant a lot of flying to and back from Arizona. I wasn't feeling flush. It had been three years since I quit my partnership and started out on my own. It takes time to grow my kind of business, especially if you don't like to make cold calls. I was doing OK, but didn't have much money in my bank accounts — barely the six months of living expenses that consultants are told to hold in reserve. I had a retirement account and could dip into it if need be, but I didn't like that idea. And it didn't feel right to ask my uncle to pay for my trips.

The sequence

When you're in a bind it's easy to blame others for putting you in it. One morning I was sitting in my apartment looking at my calendar. I was not in a good mood. I felt my cousin's request was unreasonable, resented her for not withdrawing it after she saw what I needed to do about it.

I got up, walked to a window and stared at a tree that grew outside it. A thought came: "This is silly. Your cousin is fighting for her life. If there's something you can do that might help her, what does it matter if to do it you have to blow your stash?"

The thought unloosened something. The feeling of being in a bind faded and disappeared. There was no longer any conflict between what I wanted to do and what I felt I ought to do. My mood brightened.

The next morning I got a call from a client in Santa Rosa. "Short notice," he said, "but any chance you could come run a few sessions for us, last half of next week and the first three days of the one after it?" Yes, I said, those dates are open.

I called Greg. Would he be there towards the end of the week after next? I told him I'd be flying back from San Francisco, could easily fly via Phoenix and drive up to Flagstaff.

Yes, he said, he'd be home. And wasn't it nice that a client was going to pay the airfare.

Turned out to also work for the client. The flight with a stop in Phoenix cost less than a nonstop from San Francisco to Boston.

I didn't get done in Santa Rosa until Thursday of the second week. I got to Phoenix around noon that Friday. I called Greg from the airport to let him know I was there and about to pick up my rental car for the drive to Flagstaff.

"You'll never believe this," he said, "There's going to be a healing ceremony in our house tonight." The medicine woman, Bella, was OK with my being in it. The timing was fortuitous. Bella happened to be around. Greg's wife, Alice, asked for the ceremony. Bella agreed to do it.

The ceremony was called Beautyway. It began at nightfall and ended the next morning at dawn. The primary focus of this one was not any one person but the household. The objective was to increase harmony among all its members. But it seemed that part of the way to do that was to also tend to the mental or physical problems of each person there, whether a member of the household or not. We were all active participants, there were no aloof observers.

Bella worked in Navajo. For those of us who didn't speak the language, Alice translated when Bella's words were for everyone in the room, and if she had questions or comments for someone like me when it was my turn to talk about a problem.

The healing ritual began and ended with what felt to me like an invocation. (Alice didn't translate.) After it was done, Bella said something to Alice who looked at me and smiled. "She says she will work with your cousin."

Later that day we talked about the timing. Bella wanted to do it four weeks later when the moon would be in a similar phase. And she felt it was best to hold it someplace other than in this house.

Greg said we could use his camp. He took me out to see it. He owned a few acres of scrubland a half-hour's drive from town. He'd built a structure on it, a round room about twenty feet across with a domed roof. I liked the feel of the place. The developers hadn't got to this area so there were no other houses nearby.

There was a problem. A central element of the ritual was a bed of hot coals that sat on a disc of packed earth about four inches thick and a couple of feet in diameter. To keep the bed bright hot it had to be replenished often from an outdoor fire pit. The person whose job it was to make the disc, called an altar, and to tend to both fires was called the fire chief. Greg had done that job for this ceremony and was willing to be the fire chief for the one for my cousin. But he was going to be away working on one of his projects at that time. Finding someone else to fill that role was going to be difficult. Whoever it was would want to check me out. Hopefully I wouldn't have to make more than one trip back.

I worked the next two days with Greg and a pan-Indian group he was affiliated with. A day after I got back to Boston I got a call from Greg. The dates of the project work had been moved. "You have your fire chief," he said.

Two days later I got a letter from an airline. I'd flown a lot on it in the past eighteen months. Inside was a note thanking me for the business, along with a coupon good for a round-trip flight anywhere in the continental U.S.

About this time I began to wonder. Was this just a lucky

run of events, like the streaks you can have playing cards or throwing dice? Or was something else going on? But I didn't want to think too much about it. When players start making shot after shot in basketball or golf they call it being in a zone. Thinking about what's going on can throw you out of it. As in sports, so perhaps with streaks in our other activities.

I described the ceremony I'd been in to my cousin. She said she was looking forward to working with Bella, kept thanking me for setting it up. I told her I worried about feeding the notion that Bella had any miraculous healing powers. Based on what I'd seen I had reason to think she could do something for my cousin's state of mind, and that might have an impact on her physical condition. Could she do more than that? I didn't know.

"But do you think that's impossible?" my cousin asked.

"Maybe not," I said, "I suppose we should go into it with an open mind. Think of it as an experiment that may work in some ways but not in others."

"Nothing to lose then," she said, "except unreasonable hopes." She smiled. "I'll keep that in mind, and if I forget it you'll remind me."

A diversion

To tell the story of what I got from the events connected to these healing rituals I've had to introduce a second story, that of my cousin who set off those events. At about this point in my account you may be wondering what working with Bella did for Indira. I'd like to conclude that story before I pick up again with the sequence.

My cousin worked with Bella not just once but twice. After the first ceremony Bella said it would be good to have a second one a month later. Once again there was an opening for the date she picked in both Greg's and my schedules. Indira's husband was a participant on both occasions, but not her father.

It was clear to both my cousin and me that in each ceremony she became aware, for the first time, of sources of psychic wounds she'd suffered as a child that had never healed. And she got some insights into what she needed to do about them.

After both the first and second rituals her blood tests showed a movement in a positive direction, but the historical chart of those tests included both ups and downs. Was this an indication of a shift from a downward to an upward trend? Perhaps, perhaps not.

My cousin lived for seven more years instead of the six to eighteen months Western medicine predicted. Were the healing ceremonies a factor? What about the other alternative treatments she followed, such as special diets? If she did ever reach any final conclusions about these questions, I never got to hear about them.

The sequence, continued

Around mid-morning of the day on which the second healing ritual was to take place Greg asked me if I wanted to go with him to collect the earth needed for the "altar." I said I would like to do that.

We got in his pickup truck and drove into the Coconino National Forest. It was a clear, still, late spring day. About a half mile into the forest I asked Greg if there were any golden eagles in the area. He said yes, but he'd seen one only a couple of times. And he took this road frequently. "So don't hold your breath," he said.

After a while the road came out of the trees into a clearing. There was a hill on our left. Ahead of us was a wide canyon. A hundred yards from its edge the road made a sharp left turn and ran alongside the canyon, hugging the hill.

A quarter mile past the turn Greg stopped the truck next to a bare patch of hillside. We got out. Greg took a spade and some black plastic garbage bags from the back of the truck and climbed a short way up on the patch. He looked down at the ground, then up at the sky. Speaking in the same voice he'd use to talk to me he thanked the powers that be for this new day. He then talked to the hill and to the things that lived on it. He explained why he needed to take some earth away from here. A few seconds of silence, then he filled the bags.

We loaded them into the back of the truck and headed back. Before we got to the turn I saw an eagle floating in the canyon not far from its edge. I mentioned it to Greg. There was a small parking area at the bend. We pulled into it and got out. The eagle was headed to our left. It banked to its right and made a wide circle that brought it back to where it was headed in our direction.

It flew to where we stood and started to circle the parking area a hundred or so feet above our heads. Soon a second eagle floated in from another direction and joined the circle, and then a third. The three may not have circled above us for more than a minute, but it felt longer. Then, one at a time, each flew off in the direction from which it had come. We watched the one that headed for the canyon become a distant speck.

We got back in the truck and drove for a while in silence. Greg broke it. "You know what Bella says. She says if you talk to your relatives the right way, sometimes they choose to respond. Tell her tonight about what happened here."

"OK," I said. It didn't seem strange that he used those words, "they ... respond." So close to the way I'd articulated the idea I needed to make seem real to me: that there is something out there that can, if deemed appropriate, respond to an individual creature's needs. I could tell myself that all the other ways in which things had fallen into place in this venture were happenstance — a bit of luck, an improbable yet still random string of events. But it was hard to say that about what I'd just seen. And there was a follow-on to it that would give me one more thing to try to explain away.

That night during a break in the ritual I found myself alone in the room with Bella and Alice. Everyone else was outside. I described our encounter with the eagles. Soon after I started talking Bella tilted her head away from me. She was listening and at the same time looking into the burning coals on the earthen altar.

When I was done she turned to Alice, giggled, and said something to her in Navajo. Alice looked amused. She looked at me and said "Money. She says money coming your way. The eagles, they are also on the dollar bill." They got up and went out for some cool night air.

I felt a bit let down. I'd expected to hear something more lofty, some revelation about the world of the spirit or of where I stood in regard to it. Ultimately I saw that this kind of feet on the ground, pragmatic interpretation of the mysteries was exactly what James had urged me to look for in my search for sources of ideas to include in my unseen order. And that it was in part the ways in which he personified this attitude that made me like and admire Greg.

The one more thing I soon needed to explain away was why the money did indeed come my way. This second healing ritual took place at the end of May. In the next six months more business came my way than in the entire previous year. I heard from old clients I hadn't been in touch with for a while, and from new ones directed to me by both colleagues and customers.

Questions and a way to answer some of them

The ceremonies and the events related to them left me with two sets of questions that I found hard to leave unanswered.

One set was about the ceremonies. I felt I had seen only a small part of what Bella did in them. There was an element in them of group therapy run by someone with a remarkable ability to tune into what was going on in our psyches. It produced some ahas and perhaps this was all the rituals were designed to do. But I didn't think so. If I was right, what else was going on in them that I'd missed? Was there a premise with which Bella was working? If so, what?

The other set of questions had to do with the events associated with the ceremonies. One subset of these was about what the eagles did, the other about the rest of that chain of events. The second bit was the hardest to deal with so I'll start with it.

What to make of that chain of events? Was it no more than an accidental falling into place of things that helped me to do a task? After all these years I still don't have any definitive answers. But the idea that there might have been some kind of principle at work here feels plausible enough to have become a provisional element of my unseen order. What gained it that entrance was in part some speculations about how the principle could have arisen. But the deciding factor was how I felt about things as they were unfolding.

I'll describe my speculations though I doubt any amount and kind of thinking — mine or yours — will help push the idea past your threshold of acceptability. In my case that push had to come from the experience, from what I felt was happening when it happened. But the thinking I did could be helpful in another way.

We see what we are prepared to see. I may well have encountered similar strings of events before but didn't see them for what they might be because my head didn't have any place in it for that possibility. And so I didn't hear what, if anything, my intuition might have had to say about them.

The possibility

"[A] dominant theme in all Native American cultures," says Joseph Epes Brown[2], "is that of relationship, or a series of relationships that are always reaching further and further out: [from those] within the immediate family [to] the extended family [to the band, the clan, the tribe]."

The sense of being related doesn't stop there but extends out "to the land, to the animals, to the plants, and to the clouds, the elements, the heavens, the stars; and ultimately [embraces the] entire universe."

Associated with this sense of relationships, says Brown, is "the theme of reciprocity which permeates so many aspects of North American cultures." Central to the meaning of the word is the notion of a "process wherein if you receive or take away you must also give back," because by doing so you don't break the "cycle permeating all of life." Everything "comes back upon itself."

Could these notions be grounded in an intuitive grasp of how things really are in the natural world? If not out there among the stars, at least here on this earth?

Two professors, one of chemistry (Robert Shapiro) and the other of physics (Gerald Feinberg), teamed up to write the book *Life Beyond Earth*.[3] It exemplifies how to use known "hard facts" as a launchpad for imagining how things might be in the unknown. The writers tried, unsuccessfully, to convince NASA to widen its search for extraterrestrial life, to not restrict it to looking for our kind of carbon-based critters. They make a plausible case for how life could exist in all kinds of environments — including frigid ones where the air lacks oxygen and the seas are liquid ammonia, and super-hot ones "where seas of lava flow between hills of quartz [in which] silicate beings thrive."

They begin by looking at life here, from down at the level of the organisms that live and work in our cells all the way up to that of the biosphere, in which they include all "living things [plus] the part of the non-living realm that enters into their metabolic activity." Such as molecules of oxygen or iron or calcium or water.

One thing that becomes clear to them is that "the pattern of cycles within the biosphere is an interesting parallel to the complex biochemical cycles that go on within individual cells and organisms. [The] metabolism of a cell involves a long series of chemical reactions [that] influence one another."

These reactions and the organisms that carry them out "are arranged so that a product of one reaction is an essential component of another reaction. It is this interrelated set of processes that constitutes the life of a cell." And determines its state of health.

The same kind of thing happens in multicellular organisms. Here again

> there are cycles in which one part of the organism influences other parts through hormones or through nerve impulses. These processes in turn are influenced by yet other parts in a way that maintains the organism over a long period of time.

At every stage of these processes individual organisms "eat" a part of their environment and use what they take in to produce "food" for some other part of the larger organism in which they both live. The health of the host and of each creature for which it is home depends on whether the proper balance is maintained, at every level, of what is taken in and what is, in return, given out. And this holds all the way up to the organism that is our biosphere.

> In a sense, the biosphere is to its individual parts as a complex organism is to the cells of which it is composed. Just as the cells do not "know' that they are part of an organism but are nevertheless highly constrained in their behavior by this fact, so all the myriad living things of Earth do not know that they are part of a superorganism — the biosphere — but that fact nevertheless influences their function and even the fact of their existence in countless ways.

All living things except, perhaps, Homo Sap. Capable of seeing the plan and the constraints on our behavior that promote the health of the whole and, ultimately, of our own kind. But again, unlike other organisms, also capable of breaking those rules and getting away with it, seemingly forever, but in fact for a relatively brief time in the life of the earth, at four billion years just entering mid-life. Perhaps dinosaurs and other creatures ultimately did themselves in because they too broke the rules, albeit more unwittingly.

So here are some speculations.

There are feedback loops in the biosphere, as there are in our bodies and in those of one-celled organisms. As a line of creatures — such as hominids — evolves, so do the internal feedback loops that maintain their health. But because they are a part of a larger organism and what they do has an impact on its health that bigger being has to adapt to their evolution by developing new external feedback loops that influence the behavior of the newer versions of these critters.

Jump cut to a thought from the Native American world. It took Ruth Beebe Hill almost thirty years to write *Hanta Yo*[4]. It's a fictional account of a period in the life of a Lakota band. It is based on an account of that period inscribed on bark. And on many years of studying the Lakota language and working with a traditional elder to insure the integrity of the story.

A central character, still a young boy, is troubled by some things and seeks advice from Wanagi, the band's seer. Wanagi helps, but says only what he thinks the boy can absorb. After the kid leaves he finds himself thinking about the things he hopes the boy will one day understand. (Because whom he has in mind is a boy and not a girl, the use of the word "man" in what follows felt appropriate, so I haven't messed with it.)

The seer senses that the boy is not yet ready to think about "the breath that creates life, [flowing] through the two-legged they call man, something that man, like [all] creatures, receives without asking but something upon which man, unlike the [others], shall draw upon whenever he chooses ...

> And Wanagi, staying on the trail of thoughts this youth had evoked, had pursued again the meaning in this act they call "choosing," truly the most important act known to the family of man.
>
> For who but man dares choose between that which protects and that which destroys him? The wingeds fly, nest, and sing as the life-force directs; the four-legs leap, run, or hide as the life-force compels. But skan, the life-force, neither directs nor compels man; instead man directs the force. And so he provides his own protection, looks out for himself.
>
> But man owns also the power for destroying himself, for turning the life-force toward mischief and away from good, if he so chooses.
>
> If he so chooses. But will man not hold on to something in or of his body, in or of his spirit, that dignifies him? Not something he seeks, not dream or vision, but something he owns from the beginning? Certainly he learns to recognize his familiar-voice, but [it] never forbids, never compels. The familiar-voice

> identifies truth but never demands that man act on truth; man makes that choice."

Yes, but if the life-force senses that this two-legged is prone to making choices that are harmful to the whole and, ultimately to itself, perhaps it invents feedback loops that nudge its behavior back in the other direction.

Not reward systems that this clever creature could turn into a self-serving investment scheme: give some of what you have to others because the more you give the more you are likely to get back. That would also compromise its freedom to make the wrong choices.

So not that, but perhaps a feedback system designed to awaken the critter to the nature of the world in which it lives. Gifts to others, given truly freely, promote the health of the whole and, ultimately, of their own kind. And so such acts may create ripples in a local probability function that make some things more likely to happen, things that help the gift giver to do something. A feedback loop designed not to reward the act but to remind, to make the giver aware of its importance.

A far-out idea, perhaps, but not one that would break any laws of physics or chemistry or natural selection, at least none I could think of. Could be no more than a bit of wishful thinking, a take on the nature of things based more on how I'd like it to be than on how it actually is.

But we are talking here about what to include in one's personal conception of a hidden order. The only way to settle that question is to practice the art of selfless giving and see if the world responds. Which makes it a working hypothesis that is not going to harm anyone.

The eagles

I'd answered, sufficiently for me, my main question about the sequence of events related to the healing rituals: it was possible that plain luck was not all that made them fall into place; they may have been nudged in that direction by some principle of reciprocity. That explanation applied also to what the eagles did but only in a general way. It left unanswered other questions I had about it.

What did Bella mean when she said: "If you speak to your relatives the right way, sometimes they choose to respond?" Who responds? In this case each of the three birds individually, or some collective eagle consciousness, or that of all the critters in this part of the forest?

What does it mean that whatever responds chooses to do so? That implies it can hear and understand our wishes. Pets, perhaps, because they have a big incentive to be tuned into us. But wild creatures? And is it the creatures that respond, or the life force that animates us all? Both?

I've found no definitive answers to any of these questions. The idea that every species, including us, has a collective consciousness seems reasonable.

In *The Lives of a Cell*, Lewis Thomas observes that

> [Ants and] bees and termites and social wasps seem to live two kinds of lives: they are individuals, going about the day's business without much evidence of thought for tomorrow, and they are at the same time component parts, cellular elements, in the huge, writhing, ruminating organism of the Hill, the nest, the hive. [We] don't like the notion that there can be collective societies with the capacity to behave like organisms …
>
> Still, there it is. A solitary ant, afield, cannot be considered to have much on his mind, indeed, with only a few neurons strung together by fibers, he can't be imagined to have a mind at all, much less a thought. He is more like a ganglion on legs. Four ants together, or ten, encircling a dead moth on a path, begin to look like an idea. [But it] is only when you watch the dense

> mass of thousands of ants, crowded together around the Hill, blackening the ground, that you begin to see the whole beast, and now you observe it thinking, planning, calculating. It is an intelligence, a kind of live computer, with crawling bits for its wits."[5]

Thomas adds that the "phenomenon of separate animals joining up to form an organism is not unique in insects." Larger creatures also do it. "Herring and other fish in schools are at times so closely integrated, their actions so coordinated, that they seem to be functionally a great multi-fish organism. Flocking birds [are] similarly attached, connected, synchronized."

And perhaps so are other more solitary birds and animals, albeit connected in a more diffused, more subtle way. They may be able to create a collective consciousness even though the individuals are spread out in space.

So was the "relative" that chose to put on a show for Greg and me the local union of eagles? Could it have been the collective "minds" of all living things in the area come together to form a bigger "relative"?

Perhaps some of these questions will someday be answered definitively by our scientists. I haven't seen any such answers. Until I — or you — see them, we all have to answer the questions for ourselves.

How? Again the only way I see is to take the idea on as a working hypothesis and experiment with it.

Send out a voice to some wild creatures. Address them as you would a friend and equal. See what happens. Be prepared to see no conclusive results right away. Lack of impatience could be a factor in whether or not you get a response, as could your intentions. And you may have picked a time when those relatives are preoccupied with something else.

9
The premise

> In many [Native American cultures] religion is viewed as embodying the reciprocal relationship between people and the sacred processes going on in the world. It may not involve a "god." It may not be signified by praying or asking for favors ... A Navajo goes to the equivalent of a priest to get well because one needs not only medicine, [but also] to reestablish one's relationship with the rhythms of nature.
>
> — Barre Toelken
> *Seeing with a Native Eye*[1]

I had, you may recall, two sets of questions about the healing rituals. One was, in essence, whether there was anything other than pure chance that made things go the way they did and, if so, what that might be. I've described some possible answers that I was able to use as working hypotheses.

The other set of questions was about the ceremonies. Was there anything going on in them other than a traditional version of group therapy? I felt there was another dimension to it but didn't have any idea of what it might be.

Eventually I learned that there was more to what Bella was doing. Perhaps I might have glimpsed some of it if I understood Navajo. Or if Alice or Greg had given me a mini-tutorial. But they didn't, either because they didn't think it was necessary, or because putting together an explanation would have taken more time than they could give to it.

Writers do have the time for such things. A few months after the ceremonies I came across two essays that helped me understand the premise behind what Bella was trying to do.

One was written by Barre Toelken, who was adopted by a Navajo elder, "lived an essentially Navajo life for roughly two years," and continued to go back whenever he could to be with his Navajo family.

The other was by the writer Barry Lopez, who spent big chunks of time with Native tribes. Much of it with those who live in the far North, but a significant amount with others elsewhere. I'll start with a train of thought of his that starts in "a remote village in the Brooks range of Alaska."[2]

A group of Native hunters is telling stories about their encounters with wolverines. Their accounts get Lopez thinking about how we see and work with the landscape, and that we all live in two, the exterior and the interior. He reflects on what he has learned about the two.

> The exterior landscape is the one we see. [If] you walk up, say, a dry arroyo in the Sonoran desert, you will feel a mounding and rolling of sand and silt beneath your foot that is distinctive. [In such] tangible evidence you will sense a history of water in the region. Perhaps a yellow-throated sparrow lands in a paloverde bush — the resiliency of the twig under the bird, that precise shade of yellowish-green against the milk-blue sky, [the] smell of creosote bush, [an] animal track obscured by wind.
>
> These are all elements of the land, and what makes the landscape comprehensible is the relationships between them. One learns a landscape finally not by knowing the name or identity of everything in it,

> but by perceiving the relationships in it — like that between the sparrow and the twig."

The interior landscape is "a kind of projection within a person" of the relationships perceived in the exterior landscape. These include ones that are

> named and discernible, such as the nitrogen cycle, or a vertical sequence of Ordovician limestone, and others that are uncodified or ineffable, such as winter light falling on a particular kind of granite, or the effect of humidity on the frequency of a blackpoll warbler's burst of song.

The relationships in the exterior landscape "have a purpose and order, however inscrutable they may seem to us. [Similarly] the speculations, intuitions, and formal ideas we refer to as "mind' are a set of relationships in the interior landscape." Some of these "are obvious, many impenetrably subtle." These relationships in our minds

> are deeply influenced by where on this earth one goes, what one touches, the patterns one observes in nature — the intricate history of one's life in the land, even a life in the city, where wind, the chirp of birds, the line of a falling leaf are known. [The] shape of the individual mind is affected by land as it is by genes,"

The exterior landscape, he adds,

> is organized according to principles or laws or tendencies beyond human control. It [has] an integrity that is beyond human analysis and unimpeachable. Insofar as the storyteller depicts various subtle and obvious relationships in the exterior landscape accurately [the] narrative will "ring true.' [The listeners] will find [a] sense of congruence within [themselves] and also with the world."

He recalls that among the Navajo "and, as far as I know, many other Native peoples, the land is thought to exhibit a sacred order," and rituals seek to align us with "the power in that order." We all seek to order our interior landscape to reflect the reality of the exterior. "To succeed in this means to achieve a balanced state of mental health."

He thinks of the premise of the Navajo Beautyway ceremony.

> In the Navajo view, the elements of one's interior life — one's psychological makeup and moral bearing — are subject to a persistent principle of disarray. Beautyway is, in part [an] invocation of the order of the exterior universe … The purpose of this invocation is to increase in the individual who is the subject of [the] ceremony that same order, to make the individual again a reflection of the myriad enduring relationships of the landscape.

Barre Toelken echoes this idea that a factor in our wellbeing is our conception of how things in nature relate to each other and to us. Here is one of the examples he gives of how it is kept in mind.

There's a brown bead that's found inside a blue juniper berry. "Navajos search to find where the small ground animals have hidden their supply of juniper seeds. Usually a small girl, sometimes a boy, will look for [these] hiding places." When a girl finds one she scoops out all the seeds. She doesn't want to rob the animals of their food, so she looks for the ones "that have already been broken open. [She] puts all the whole seeds back, and takes only the ones that have a hole in one end. She takes them home, cleans them, punches a hole in the other end with a needle, and strings them together."

"I do not know," Toelken adds, "any Navajo in my family or among my acquaintances who ever goes without these beads." Why?

His Navajo sister tells him that one of the things they prevent is nightmares. How so? Because

> they represent the partnership between the tree that gave its berries, the animals which gather them, and the humans who pick them up (being careful not to deprive the animals of their food.) [Thus] if you keep these beads on you and think about them, your mind, in its balance with nature, will tend to lead a healthy existence."
>
> Being healthy means, to the Navajo, that
>
> > you are participating properly in all the cycles of nature, and thus you will not have bad dreams [which] are a sign of being sick. [So] these beads are not for warding off sickness itself; rather, they are reminders of a frame of mind which [is in] the proper relationship with the rest of nature — a frame of mind necessary to the maintenance of health.
>
> And you go to a healing ritual because
>
> > to get well one needs not only medicine [but also] to reestablish one's relationship with the rhythms of nature. [The] medicine may cure the symptoms, but [not] cure you. It does not put you back in step with [the] natural cycles."

Toelken refers to the rhythms and cycles of nature as "sacred" processes. Lopez talks about the "sacred order" exhibited by the land. The label seems apt.

The word sacred is derived from the Latin *sacer*, holy. And the root of holy is *häl*, whole. The word hale also means whole, as well as "free from disease or infirmity; robust."

The rhythms and cycles and reciprocal relationships found in nature promote the wellbeing of the whole and are in that sense holy. Being mindful of them helps us be hale, as individuals and as a species. Alienating ourselves from them sickens both us and the whole that is our biosphere. Neither is well right now.

It seems that traditional healing rituals do for the psyche what certain physical exercises do for the body — line up its load-bearing parts so they work properly with the force of gravity.

I had been in three healing ceremonies. Had they, or the events related to them, done anything for my psyche? Certainly the events planted some ideas in my inner landscape that had not been there before. These, along with what I learned later about the premise of the rituals and about other aspects of the traditional worldview gave me what I needed to heal my spirit.

There were several ways in which this "medicine" worked. One was by giving me a conception of nature's "sacred" order that I could make use of in my personal life, something I could be rooted in strongly enough to not be thrown by any misfortunes that came my way. But given the nature of my angst that was not sufficient to sustain my spirit. I also needed to see how elements of that conception could be used in the modern world to deal with the ecological crisis we'd created for ourselves.

Recall that a component of my angst was loss of faith in Homo Sap., in our collective ability to act wisely in our dealings with the rest of the natural world. I had begun to suspect that there was a flaw in our makeup, a rogue gene that trumped our good sense and impelled us to do things that, deep down, we knew were ultimately self-destructive.

But the Traditionals — in North America and elsewhere — evolved a lifestyle that didn't poison the air they breathed, the water they drank, or the food they ate. They too were Homo Saps. If they weren't innately self-destructive, then neither were the rest of us. The differences in our abilities to live sustainably were rooted not in our genes but in the degree to which we, in the modern world, had gotten out of step with the rhythms and cycles of nature.

So there was no rogue gene that made us incapable of living at peace with the natural world. Only a sickness of our own making, and what we had made we could unmake. This way of thinking about our situation made me feel both more hopeful for and more kindly toward us as a species.

I had never lost my fondness for the many essentially caring individuals I knew. But I had come to think of them as exceptions, not representative of humanity as a collective entity, one that seemed incapable of behaving intelligently in its dealings with the natural world.

Disappointment breeds anger, and anger blinds us to things. The intensity of my anger had begun to abate after Maslow and Frankl helped me see that human nature included a transcendent self that cared for its world, perhaps because it understood that such caring was a key to the long-term survival of its kind. What I learned about the way of life evolved by the Traditionals helped me regain a measure of faith in the ability of Homo Sap. to be guided by that understanding.

And that, in turn, helped me to see that I'd become angry with my kind because I cared about it. My angst was an echo not only of the pain we were inflicting on the earth, but as much if not more of the pain I could see we were going to inflict on our now and future children. The earth had ways of healing itself and would endure; it was we who might not.

A goal of traditional healing ceremonies was to help participants to become aligned — or realigned — with the laws and principles and forces that work to maintain the health of our ecosystem as a whole. Was there some way to increase the degree of that alignment in the thoughts and acts of people who live in the modern world?

If it could be done it would enhance our ability to create a more sustainable way of living and, in the process, avoid or soften the impact of the earth's reactions to the damage we've done to it. This could happen in two ways, one more mundane than the other.

The more ordinary one is that we'd be better informed about how the natural world works. The more complete your picture of a situation, the more likely that your response to it will be productive, whether these responses be changes in how we want to live or in the way we deploy our technology.

The more far-out possibility is that our attempt to increase our alignment with the natural order might incline the forces associated with it to give us some assists. Merely acknowledging their existence and asking for help may evoke no response if we hold to our unsustainable lifestyle. But sincere efforts to change it might do it.

To get any comfort from these ideas I had to be able to imagine how the alignment could happen. It would require a big shift in our dominant conception of the natural world and of how to live in it. That shift has already begun but only in the minds and acts of a small number of people in the modern world, including some eminent scientists.

But to make any difference the shift in our stance toward nature needs to move from the fringes of our society to its middle, enough so to influence the thinking of our political and business leaders. In the past such movements have occurred very slowly. But I fear that we don't have a lot of time for it. Perhaps one or two generations, possibly three. The speed of change in our eco-system has picked up and we need to keep pace with it to survive. Or at least to not be mauled too badly by those changes.

Is there any hope that we can shift, quickly enough, our operating stance toward the natural world? It's hard to loosen the grip of old habits and of those with big stakes in keeping things as they are. But it is also possible to see how these powerful forces could be neutralized, to imagine a way forward.

It would need to be a way forward that did not require others to incorporate any part of my personal unseen order into their conceptions of reality. It's hard enough to get people to reconsider their perception of the observable aspects of the natural world. Asking them to also tinker with what they consider to be their religious — or anti-religious — views would make it an almost impossible task. And one of which I would want no part.

Some of you may nevertheless want to know what's in my picture of the hidden world. I will talk about it soon, but only after I've described a way forward for which knowledge of its details is not a prerequisite.

10
Pruning the interior landscape

Human history is, in essence, the history of ideas.
— H.G. Wells[1]

The need for work at the root level

Donald Kaufman is the Director of Miami University's Center for Environmental Education. He and co-author Cecilia Franz put together a big (almost 500-page) textbook titled *The Biosphere: Protecting our Global Environment.*[2] It provides a comprehensive overview of the subject, rather than a detailed look at any one aspect of it. The broad view enables one to see how any one effort to deal with an environmental issue meshes — or doesn't mesh — with others.

How does the alignment task I'm talking about here relate to the many other things people are doing or thinking of doing about our eco-problems? At the causal level, it can be seen as an enabler for all of them.

There are, the authors note, three "root causes" of environmental problems. These are "population growth, abuse of resources and natural systems, and pollution."

And what, at a deeper level, is the common ground in which these three causes are, in turn, rooted?

It's our "attitudes, values, and beliefs." These "comprise a person's *worldview* — a way of perceiving reality that includes basic assumptions about the self, others, nature, space, and time. An important part of any worldview is a person's beliefs about the role of humans in the natural world." Those attitudes toward nature and the environment lead to behaviors that can either cause or minimize environmental problems."

Our values and ideas about the nature of things are "reflected in and transmitted through culture." Our culture, I would add, is something we are immersed in from the day we are born (and perhaps even before that). Much of the time we take in its constructs and mores as unwittingly as we breathe in what's in our air. No need to examine those concepts more critically if our culture's survival strategy seems sound. But when there's an ever-increasing flow of evidence that questions the wisdom of that strategy, it's time to do some conceptual house cleaning, to make the ideas that shape our "attitudes toward nature" more congruent with its "sacred" order.

Imagining a way forward

> Stories entertain and they instruct. They delight and they teach. Stories work best when they are told either to the very young or to those who have not forgotten the child within them, who open themselves without preconceptions to the possibility of other worlds than their own everyday reality, who accept that even everyday life — if seen through different eyes — may be suffused with magic.
>
> — Joseph Bruchac
> *I Become Part of It*[3]

Changing our perception of the natural world* involves changing the stories we tell ourselves about it. The storytellers who have the most authority in the modern world are our scientists. Does looking to the Traditionals for some of our stories mean moving away from those told by Science? Not for some of the ones I think would increase our alignment with the natural order. Because in these our science is beginning to say the same things about the natural world that the Traditionals hold are true.

What these stories say about how things are in that world may not be news to you. The ideas about it that they convey have been around for a while in the modern world. But they have taken root only in the fringes of its collective consciousness. I throw them out again here in the hope that they will float, like milkweed seed puffs, and get deposited in the minds of those most capable of transplanting them in the popular imagination. And of doing that more quickly than could be done by anyone else.

Who are these people? The gifted storytellers among us: novelists, moviemakers, cartoonists, choreographers, rappers, poets, painters, singers of folksongs. Especially the young ones of this and the next few generations. Because they have a bigger stake in the future than their elders, and because they are more adept at using the electronic stages that make the whole world their audience. And for the reasons given below.

How we choose to live is determined by what we believe the nature of things to be. So increasing our alignment with the natural order has to begin with changes in our conception of it. But the job isn't done until those changes are reflected in the way we act. It's not hard to see that getting aligned will mean shifting from a high to a much

---

* I use the terms "external landscape," "natural world," and "nature" interchangeably, to mean that part of our world that exists independently of the one that is our creation, conceptually or physically. The one that was there before we were, and that will be there after we're gone.

lower consumption lifestyle. Making that transition will not be easy. Imagine the turmoil in the world's stock markets if China — or any other economic power — suddenly announced a ten-year plan to cut in half its usage of raw materials. To do something like that even over a span of several generations will require big innovations, if we don't want the shift to be too traumatic.

We can't go back to the Traditional way of life even if we wanted to do it; there isn't enough room left for it. We will need to invent a new concept of the good life, and create a different kind of economy. The changes will be resisted mightily by those whose power flows from the current order, and by those who find new ideas scary.

Who better to take on these challenges than the young ones of this and future generations? I think they can do it, and I'll say a bit later about why I think so. But let's talk first about the first part of the storytellers' task: how to retell some truths about nature in ways that engage the imaginations and stir the souls of their audiences.

Recall that the purpose of a traditional healing ceremony is to invoke "the order of the exterior universe" and thereby help participants' psyches to reflect that reality. Our gifted storytellers can be the modern world's equivalents of the medicine men and women who conduct those ceremonies.

Like most basic truths the ones they need to invoke are mundane, in both senses of the word: "of or pertaining to the earth," and "common, ordinary, unimaginative." Ho-hum. But if taken to heart by enough people they have the power to move us in a big way, away from making war on nature to living at peace with it. So they must be told. The challenge is to do so in ways that make them feel urgent and compelling. That will require a large measure of creativity.

It's not a state of war out there

> [Darwin and some of his followers] overstressed and misunderstood the factor of competition and either largely or altogether neglected and underestimated the factor of co-operation. They failed to give the [latter] a place in the concept of natural selection in particular and in the description of the evolutionary process in general. In [so doing] they succeeded in conveying a view of nature that was badly maimed and sadly out of focus.
>
> — Ashley Montagu,
> *Darwin: Competition and Cooperation*[4]

We cannot grasp the essence of the natural world, as Lopez reminds us, only by "knowing the name or identity of everything in it." We also have to see clearly the relationships that exist between its elements. Our ideas about these relationships, whether or not held consciously, are revealed by the words we use to describe them.

A predator is "a predatory person, organism, or thing." The Latin root, *praedator*, means plunderer. And to plunder is to "take wrongfully, as by pillage, robbery, or fraud," or to take "by open force, as in war, hostile raids, brigandage, etc." Examples of using the word include, in my dictionary, "to plunder a town," and "to plunder the public treasury." Synonyms include rape, ravage, sack, devastate.

"Prey" is defined as "an animal hunted or seized for food," and also "a person or thing that is the victim of an enemy, a swindler, a disease, or the like." The archaic meaning is "booty or plunder." its Latin root, *praeda*, is the twin of that of the booty-taker. There is a whiff of wrongdoing and ill will toward the victim in the verb sense of the word. "To prey" means not only to do the hunting or looting ("The Vikings preyed on coastal settlements"), but also "to exert a harmful or destructive influence (*His worries preyed upon his mind*)."

So every time we call some of our fellow creatures "predators" and others their "prey," we imply that their relationship is essentially that of rapacious killers and their hapless victims. Those two words are everywhere in our talk about the natural world, whether in TV documentaries, or in the pages of magazines such as *National Geographic* and *Nature*, or in everyday conversations about the subject. The implication is reinforced by images, on screen or in our heads, such as those of a cheetah chasing down and ripping into a Grant's gazelle, or an eagle grabbing and tearing up a bunny rabbit. A merciless game of natural selection in which the ruthless predators are destined to be the eaters, their innocent prey the eaten. The rules of the game say that cunning and might make right.

Is that really how it is in the natural world or is that picture a projection onto it of how it is in the one we've created? Some of our scientists would say it's the latter. So would those who had or still have a much closer relationship with nature than do most of us who live in the modern world. Here are some ways in which they see and experience things.

A face-off in the Kalahari desert

Elizabeth Marshall Thomas, her brother John (whom I got to know), and their parents spent a lot of time in the 1950s with some clans of Bushmen who lived in the Kalahari desert. They were the first Westerners to make contact with them. *The Harmless People*[5] is one of the books Elizabeth wrote about that experience. She tells of an occasion on which John accompanied three Bushmen on a hunt. "They were tracking a bull wildebeest that one of the hunters had shot. They came upon it lying down, surrounded by a very large pride of lions." There were around twenty or thirty of them. The wildebeest was still capable of doing damage with its horns. Several lions stood near it, looking for a way to move in on it. The others paced behind some nearby bushes.

> The bushmen had followed the wildebeest's trail through thorns and over parching desert and were not to be deprived, and, speaking softly to the lions they said: 'We know you are strong, Big Lions, we know you are brave, but this meat is ours, and you must give it back to us.' [The] lions did not give ground. Their round eyes watched the hunters and they began to growl.

The hunters had a few arrows left, and one spear. They knew it would be foolish to try to use them. "[They said again], respectfully, "Great lions, Old Lions, this meat belongs to us," and then advanced on the lions, [tossing] little stones and clods of dirt.

The ones near the wildebeest stood their ground until a clod struck one of them, causing it to "huff and run back a little." That seemed to be a signal to the others that the matter was settled. The ones in the bushes had perhaps sensed how it was going to end and begun moving away even before that moment. Now all those facing the hunters turned and ran to catch up with them. The hunters still had some work to do with the wildebeest, but the lions left them to it.

Could I have found the courage to do what the Bushmen did in similar circumstances? Perhaps, if I could see lions through their eyes. But for sure I — and likely you — wouldn't try that approach in an analogous situation in a big city: You come out of a shopping mall and head for your car. It's parked in a far corner of the lot. Only a few cars left in it this late in the day.

When you are about thirty yards away from it you see four or five tough-looking guys around your car. They've broken into it, taken some things out and are rummaging in it for more to take. There's no one else in the lot. Knowing what you do about life in the big city you don't consider confronting them. You don't even use your phone to call the cops until you've turned around and put a few more yards between you and the ruffians.

I don't mean to imply that you can't get robbed in the wild. Bears and raccoons will eat your lunch and dinner if they can. And you can't wander about in it without keeping in mind that for some critters you are the equivalent of a lovely ripe tomato. But what's not there is malice. And if there's an instinct that makes us respect the rights of others, it seems to manifest itself more often in that world than in ours.

Alice and the bees

Rolling Thunder was a Cherokee medicine man. He is the subject of a book named after him and written by Doug Boyd, a member of the research department of the Menninger Foundation.[6] R. T. (as he let himself be called when I met him) agreed to let Boyd hang around as he went about some of his work.

R. T. still performed some healing rituals for individuals, but much of his time was spent on issues related to Indian rights. Such as trying to prevent the bulldozing of thousands of acres of pinyon forests on treaty lands administered by the Bureau of Land Management. At first Boyd's task was to listen and observe without getting in the way. But soon he became part of a group of non-Indians who helped R. T. with some of these projects.

R. T. lived in a house at the edge of a small town in Nevada. When Boyd and any other helpers needed to be at hand they usually camped in a secluded spot in the nearby hills. R. T. often came to gather medicinal plants that grew in the area. He was sometimes joined by Alice, a woman older and more straight-laced than the others in Boyd's group.

Boyd describes her as "A middle-aged white woman from Salt Lake City [with] right-wing political views, for which ailments Rolling Thunder gave her occasional treatments." So why did she hang out with R. T.? Because "she was also a chemist and experienced herbalist," and they helped each other identify and find uses for medicinal plants.

After one herb-gathering trip with R. T., Boyd recounts,

> Alice came down the path toward me, walking very fast. "I want to tell you something,' she puffed, "It couldn't have happened without Rolling Thunder, I know, but I actually communicated with the bees. [I] talked to them and they understood.

She said R.T. told her to tell Boyd what happened because it was his job to write about such things. They had gone to get horehound plants.

> Rolling Thunder knew right where they were. [But] I saw that the plants were absolutely covered with bees. I'm deathly afraid of bees, it frightens me just to look at them and they always sting me. [So] I was just ready to leave. [Well] Rolling Thunder talked to me, he was so kind and gentle. He sensed what I was feeling, [he] told me I was really not afraid of animals or any living thing, I only thought I was ... He told me that [such fears] are based on misunderstanding.
>
> He said "Now Alice, I want you to talk to those bees. I saw how you talked to the dogs [at the camp who needed help]. You talked to the babies and the mother and you said the right things in the right way. If you can talk to dogs that way you can talk to bees, and they will understand, [not] the English language, but your meaning.

> So he told me [to] ask the bees to share the plants with me, to tell them I wouldn't harm them and to explain that I needed the plants for good medicine, but I would leave enough for the bees and for seeds for the coming year. He told me to say it loud and clear. [I did] as he said, and, do you know, the bees actually understood me, and they moved! I just can't describe how I felt. All the bees on the plant I was looking at moved. They all moved together to the back of the plant. I took only from the front half of the plant which they had left [for me].

She says that she then moved to another plant covered with bees:

> And the same thing happened again! On one of the plants, when the bees moved back and I started to cut, they all made the strangest buzzing sound [as though they were] telling me to stop, and I was understanding. I looked at Rolling Thunder and he said, "There now, you see? You and the bees have agreed to share and now you're cutting back too far. They'll expect you, now, to do as you said." So I cut only from the front half very carefully.

She added that when she was done Rolling Thunder said that she had just been given a gift, and not by him. Boyd notes that she seemed "filled with emotion" when she said this. "Immediately she turned and walked back along the path as quickly as she had come."

I've never needed to pluck something from a plant covered with bees. But I have often watched a couple of bees, a few flower-flies, and a bumblebee working in tight quarters, either on a single flower or on a small cluster of them. They move around but there's no bumping or shoving that I can see. The bumblebee looks huge next to the littlest of the flower-flies. It has a sting, they don't. But it seems content to share the goodies with them.

Every time I see this one-act play I wonder if I'm glimpsing an aspect of nature's "sacred" order, something in it that informs its critters that they are supposed to share its gifts with others, regardless of how plentiful or scarce they are.

Doesn't mean they all do it all the time. It seems that nature's rules aren't rigid: it's OK if they are followed most of the time but not always. Wolves will pay no heed to foxes watching them eat an elk they've killed, waiting for their chance at what is left uneaten. But on occasion the wolves react differently — one or two of them will go after one of those foxes and kill it.

It would make sense for nature's order to have flexibility built into it, to allow for variations in ability and temperament among the individuals in any tribe of critters. It would be hard for natural selection to do its work without those variations.

Wilderness — more than just a pretty face

> The role of wilderness and wild lands in preventing climate change is not receiving nearly the attention from the international community that it needs to.
>
> — From a post by the WILD Foundation[7]

In an article in the *International Journal of Wilderness*, Harvey Locke and Brendan Mackay note that

> Recent scientific research has shown clearly that protecting primary ecosystems such as forests, wetlands, and peatlands (whether they be tropical, temperate, or boreal) is a necessary part of solving the climate change problem."[8]

Why? Two reasons, the authors say. These are:

- The impact on carbon dioxide emissions. "[Though] 70% of the total historic increase in greenhouse gas levels in the atmosphere due to human activity is from burning fossil fuel, [about] 30% is from deforestation." There is the equivalent of 7 trillion tons of carbon dioxide stored in forests and other terrestrial ecosystems such as wetlands and peatlands, "[and we] are depleting these green carbon stocks and releasing the carbon dioxide into the atmosphere at an alarming rate."

- Impact on the ecosystem's ability to adapt to the "harmful climate change [that] is now unavoidable." That change "will place stress on ecosystems and the environmental services they provide, especially the provision of food and freshwater. Many communities, especially in poorer countries, will be affected. Intact, natural ecosystems with their biodiversity fully functioning are more resilient to stresses than degraded lands. Healthy ecosystems will prove [to be] an invaluable resource in helping [us] adapt to unavoidable climate change."

What can be done to preserve and even add to our stock of wilderness areas? The authors focus on the need to work at the institutional level — that of government policies and international protocols such as the "Convention on Biological Diversity" or the U.N.'s "Framework Convention on Climate Change."

This work, the authors say, "is necessary but not sufficient. There is a pressing higher-level need for politicians and NGOs[†] to show leadership in recognizing that the climate change problem, the biodiversity extinction crisis, and the destruction of wilderness have the same root cause and that coordinated, holistic solutions are required."

Yes, but most politicians aren't leaders, they are led by their sense of where their voters are (and if they are autocrats, of where their potential troublemakers are). So I would add that there is also a pressing *lower*-level need to

† Non-Governmental Organizations

shift the general public's attitudes toward wilderness. Too many people still see it as an enemy to be conquered and feared, even though it has its uses for hunting and fishing and fun vacations.

The need to do some work on the popular imagination is recognized by the authors of a U.S. Geological Survey "Supply Paper."[9] They review some of the benefits wetlands provide, such as minimizing damage from floods, purifying water that flows through them, and sequestering carbon. They say, in their conclusions, that "If any hope remains for preserving the Nation's wetland resources, it depends upon obtaining public support." But they assume, as the authors of such papers tend to do, that "Public support can be won if scientists can explain clearly how wetlands function, how they interact with their surroundings, and how their functions can benefit society."

To which I would add "necessary, but not sufficient." Facts, by themselves, seldom capture imaginations. But stories based on them can. Stories need central characters. For at least some about the wilderness, I'd nominate the wolf.

The Character

> The fairy tales have it wrong; large [carnivores] are our friends. To be healthy our world needs them.
>
> — John Carter
> *Nature Trails*, Volume 45, Number 8[10]

Barry Lopez, whom I quoted earlier, is also the author of a book about wolves.[11] Part 1 is descriptive. Part 2 looks at how the Inuit and other North American tribes perceived and related to the animal. Part 3, "The Beast of Waste and Desolation," is a search for the origins of the intense hatred that many from the Old World felt and still feel toward wolves.

"The hatred," he says, "has religious roots: the wolf was the Devil in disguise. And it has secular roots: wolves killed stock and made men poor. At a more general level it had to do, historically, with feelings about wilderness. What men said about the one, they generally meant about the other. To celebrate wilderness was to celebrate the wolf; to want an end to wilderness and all it stood for was to want the wolf's head."

So the wolf will play a role in our stories about wilderness whether or not it appears on stage. In our minds it lurks in the wings.

The wilderness is getting good press. There is an increasing amount of talk about how it can promote our wellbeing. But its embodiment, the wolf, still evokes negative feelings in many people and more needs to be done about that, despite the evidence that it may be impossible for some of those folks to let go of those feelings.

David Mech, a wildlife biologist who studied wolves intensively and has also written books about them, has come across people like that. Mech writes

> Unfortunately, there still exists in certain segments of human society an attitude that any animal (except man) that kills another is a murderer. To these people the wolf is a most undesirable creature. "They're all dirty killers," is the way one Minnesota state representative expressed this attitude.[12]

He adds,

> These people cannot be changed. If the wolf is to survive, the wolf haters must be outnumbered. They must be outshouted, out-financed, and outvoted. Their narrow and biased attitude must be outweighed by [one that is] based on an understanding of natural processes. Finally, their hate must be outdone by a love for the whole of nature, for the unspoiled wilderness, and for the wolf as a beautiful, interesting, and integral part of both.

So what are some truths about wolves that we can shout out in song and dance and bedtime story? Here are a few.

The wolf, the elk, and the aspens

Wolves, it seems, are less like dirty killers than like another endangered species, your dedicated family physician. Bill Ripple is a researcher at Oregon State University's College of Forestry. He and a colleague published a paper in which they describe what they found in a study of the effects of reintroducing wolves into Yellowstone National Park.

Removal of the wolves from Yellowstone and other Parks "had resulted in an abnormal increase" in the numbers of elk and deer and "accelerated range destruction." In their absence the elk population had grown, accompanied by a significant "reduction or loss of woody browse species," including willows, cottonwoods, and aspens.[13]

The elks, unchecked, were destroying their habitat. The return of the wolves brought the elk population down to a more sustainable level and began a recovery of the "browse species." Or, as the *New York Times* put it, "Yellowstone's Wolves Save Its Aspens." Not a surprise ending, perhaps, but there were a couple of unexpected twists in the story.

One was that the presence of wolves had an impact not only by reducing the number of elk but also by changing their behavior. An article about Ripple's work notes that "The rapid recovery of aspens, willows, and cottonwoods [seemed] to be greater in magnitude than could be accounted for just by wolves killing elks."[14] The elk were more vigilant, they moved around more, didn't hang around in one place until they'd eaten every young shoot they could find. I couldn't help thinking: hey, less splurging and more exercising can't be bad for them.

What was definitely good for the Park was that the elk

also "shied away from zones along a stream where there their getaway would be tough because of a steep bank, or deep water, and in these zones the plants' recovery was the most rapid."

The second twist in the story was one that might not have surprised Ripple and other researchers, but was news to me. And this was the number of other ways in which the presence of the wolves promoted the health of the Park's eco-system. Ripple notes that in their absence, in Yellowstone and other Parks, "degradation of stream-side vegetation by wild ungulates [appears] to have initiated a period of accelerated streambank and channel erosion."

Over time, that erosion has a big impact on "the character and functioning of riverine systems and increasingly limits their capability to recover. As channels become over-widened [the] frequency of overbank flows decreases — a feedback mechanism that reduces the capability of high flows to sustain any riparian plant communities that remain."

Not the end of the story. Those plant communities "are important sources of wood, leaves, dissolved organic carbon, and nutrients for aquatic ecosystems." And though "[streamside] areas typically occupy a small proportion of a given catchment, they [are] biodiversity "hotspots' not only because of the diversity of native plants [but] because they also provide habitat and food-web support for a large number of terrestrial and aquatic species." These include "flowers, lizards, amphibians, and butterflies."

Researchers have also found that killing off wolves has "a negative impact on songbird diversity and abundance." I can imagine all these plants and critters saying "please, doctor wolf, don't go away."

The picture of wolves that scientists sketch is consistent with the one that the Inuit have of them and of their relationship to the ungulates they hunt: "They are one, for the caribou feeds the wolf, but it is the wolf that keeps the caribou strong."[15]

Other carnivores such as grizzlies and cougars promote the health of wilderness systems in similar ways. Ditto for sharks in their milieu. They also belong in our stories, not as outlaws but as members of the sheriff's posse.

Coda

David Mech, whom I quoted earlier, is a wolf expert highly regarded by his peers. He noted that

> Although only a tiny fraction of the human race has ever had any direct experience with the wolf, many people in the advanced societies of the Northern Hemisphere have a definite attitude toward it, because the wolf has long been featured in folklore and fairy tales [and] in most of these fanciful accounts the animal is viewed as an outright villain, or at least a creature possessing evil tendencies.

And, he adds,

> Modern day cartoons and comic strips help maintain this attitude among the public. Unfortunately this is the only way the bulk of humanity learns about the wolf, so there is no choice for most people but to view the wolf as evil incarnate.

Mech said this in 1970. Farley Mowat's book, *Never Cry Wolf*, published seven years earlier, was then perhaps the only book (now a movie) aimed at a lay audience that tried to cast a kinder light on the creature. Mech, like most wolf researchers, thinks Mowat's book is "basically fiction founded somewhat on facts." But he grants that although "*Never Cry Wolf* does present a somewhat different view of the wolf than that seen by the scientist, it has served to stir the public from its apathy regarding the plight of the wolf."

Mech doesn't say in what ways Mowat's view is different

from that of the scientists. For sure all of Mowat's study wasn't — and doesn't claim to have been — conducted scientifically. He spent a limited amount of time watching a few wolves in the wild. And he includes in his account things the Inuit say about them that may be more figuratively than literally true. And he has an agenda, doesn't try to conceal it. He wants to "stir the public." Compared with the picture of the wolf that emerges from Mech's account, the one painted by Mowat seems a lot fuzzier and quite incomplete. But there's not much difference in the sense of the animal that I got from the two accounts.

Mowat's book is still out there, but it's no longer the only one telling a different story about wolves than the old fairy tales. But those tales are also still around. And the majority of the wolf-friendly publications (including more recent books by Mech) are likely to be read by people who already are their friends.

Since Mech first wrote about the irredeemable wolf haters, their number, as a percentage of the population, may have decreased and that of those who celebrate wolves grown. But from what I read and hear it seems that many more people still live in the middle. They have a negative view of the wolf, but could be persuaded to let it go. So there's a need for stories that speak to people who aren't part of the choir.

Recall that for many people the wolf epitomizes the wilderness. How they feel about the one is how they feel about the other. So the stories need to be told not only on behalf of the wolf (or some other feared embodiment of the wild).

Snapshots

The stories that leave me with a residue of good feeling, whether about people or about other creatures, are the ones that focus on attributes they have that I can admire. What are some that wolves possess? Here are a few.‡

- "Probably the creature's strongest personality trait is its capacity for making emotional attachments to other individuals [including humans]."(a)
- The wolf's "stamina, the way he moved smoothly and silently across the landscape."(b)
- "The wolf was also held in high regard because, though he was a fiercely loyal familial animal, he was also one who took the role of provider for the larger community. [The Hidatsa speak of] the "Invitation Song' of the wolf — the howl the wolf used to call coyotes, foxes, and magpies to the remains of his kill."(b)
- A reluctant warrior. Will go after wolves it considers intruders or grizzlies that near its den. But has a "basic aversion to fighting. [One researcher] described a tame wolf becoming "frantically upset' at witnessing its first dogfight. The wolf finally broke up the fight by pulling the aggressor off by the tail."(a)
- "[The wolf is] a beautiful beast, shy and strong, wild and free. [If] it had no other worth at all, [many] would fight to preserve it on these grounds alone."(a)

‡ (a): David Mech, op. cit. (b): Barry Lopez, op. cit.

11
Speeding the shift

> [We] must learn to grow in different ways than with our current hyper-consumption. What we now call economic 'growth' amounts too often to a Great Recession for the web of life we depend on … To accommodate the current Western lifestyle for 9 billion people, we'd need several more planets. With [many] striving to attain [that way of life we need to] redefine it — and pioneer a modest, renewable, mindful, and less material lifestyle.
>
> — Paul Crutzen and Christian Schwägerl
> *Living in the Anthropocene*[1]

The harder part of the task

Part of the task of increasing our alignment with the natural world is to counter popular misconceptions about it. Not an easy task because the mindset that creates those distortions has deep cultural roots. The other, perhaps harder, part is to change the "behaviors [that] cause environmental problems."

There are lots of ideas around about what each of us can do to help solve these problems, or at least to not make them worse. You can find them in books such as *50 Things You Can Do To Save The Earth*, or in journals such as *In Context* ("101 Ways To Heal The Earth").

Everything on such lists is something that needs to be done (don't buy aerosols, start a climate change study group, work with an organization to save a wetland or to promote electric cars, or to "deepen connection between ecology and faith"). If done by enough people for long enough these efforts could slow down the rate at which we are using up natural resources and poisoning the earth and our own bodies.

There are also many ideas about what can be done by nations and other institutions, and some of these are being implemented.

In a paper titled *Climate Change: How the World is Responding*, Joseph DiMento and Pamela Doughman note that "Between 1997 and November 2004, many of the 124 countries that had already ratified, accepted, approved, or acceded to the Kyoto Protocol began working to comply to their commitments [to reduce their greenhouse gas emissions] without waiting for the holdouts."[2]

The holdouts include the U.S., but even here "many state governments and cities have passed laws or adopted policies addressing this issue."

In addition to the things that are already being done at this level some scientists have proposed some far-out "geoengineering" fixes. James Lovelock lists some of these in one of his "Gaia" books.[3]

One is "the use of a sun-shade [placed] in orbit around the sun and in synchrony with the motion of the earth." Made of "fine carbon-fiber mesh [spun] into a disk ten or more miles in diameter, [it] would disperse a few percent of the sunlight incident upon the earth." Other ideas include increasing the earth's reflectivity by "introducing [tons of] sulphuric acid droplets into the stratosphere," or by creating "the artificial equivalent of [low-flying] marine stratus clouds."

Lovelock adds that all these ideas for offsetting global heating "are no cures, since carbon dioxide would continue to increase and do damage in ways other than heating, but they [could] provide a stay of execution while a more permanent treatment is developed."

The same thing could be said about technologies that do reduce CO_2 emissions but not other kinds of pollution or the rate at which we are destroying the natural world.

Ditto for most of the more mundane ideas about what individuals and nations can or are doing about our eco-problems. I doubt there's any "permanent treatment" that doesn't address the root cause of those problems: our "hyper-consumption" way of life.

What can our storytellers do to facilitate a shift to a more "mindful and less material" lifestyle? Work with those ideas — their own or those of others — that do address the root cause. What follows are examples of things that can and are being done about it.

Redefining the good life

> Simplicity of living, if deliberately chosen, implies a compassionate approach to life. It means we are choosing to live [with] some degree of conscious appreciation of the condition of the rest of the world.
>
> — Duane Elgin
> *Voluntary Simplicity*[4]

This is the area in which there seems to be more going on at the grassroots level than in the ones I talk about later. These ongoing movements include:

New variations on old themes

"The idea that achieving ever-higher levels of consumption [is] a vacuous goal," notes the sociologist Amitai Etzioni, "has been around from the onset of industrialization." And that idea has spawned "many alternative approaches to life" in capitalist economies ... One such approach, referred to by its adherents as voluntary simplicity, has been steadily gaining in popularity."[5]

There are many different manifestations of this movement, but they all involve "the decision to limit expenditures on consumer goods and services and to cultivate nonmaterialistic sources of satisfaction and meaning, out of free will rather than out of coercion by poverty [or government programs.]"

Why would people wish to live with less stuff? Perhaps because the idea of letting go of material symbols of success feels liberating. Or because they think it's the environmentally responsible thing to do. Or for some other reason. Whatever the motivation, their numbers seem to be growing.

Etzioni cites a study[5] whose authors found that "the percentage of [U.S.] respondents with clear postmaterialist values doubled from 9 percent in 1972 to 18 percent in 1991, while those with clear materialist values dropped by more than half, from 35 percent to 16 percent. [Trends] were similar for most Western European countries."[6] I would guess a similar trend would be seen among the wealthier segments of people in less developed economies.

OK, but spending on personal consumption continued to grow. It increased by fifty percent — "real dollars" — between 1980 and 1994, and consumer debt "rose from approximately $350 billion in 1980 to $1.231 trillion in 1997."

So there seems to be a disconnect between people's wish to make do with less stuff and their ability to let it go.

"What is needed," Etzioni says elsewhere, "is to help people realize that contained consumption [is] not a reflection of failure. It is rather the liberation [from] an obsession [that equates extravagant consumption with success.] … Thus those who always wanted a modest wedding [and choose to not have a lavish one] need to be held up as a model for sensible conduct. [Once] only the nouveau riche displayed their wealth by dressing up. Dressing down [as old money did] must once again become a source of communal [approval and an] expression of a new lifestyle [lauded] by a new normative culture."[7]

Here, then, is one task for our storytellers: find the heroes and heroines you need for your songs and stories among those who choose to live with less stuff.

The Center for a New American Dream

The aims of this Center include those embraced by the voluntary simplicity movement, but extend beyond them. It also envisions a "life beyond overconsumption, disposable lifestyles, and perpetual marketing." And it wants to help people redefine the "good life" as one that is less addicted to stuff and more ecologically sustainable.

But these themes are threads in a larger tapestry, elements of a larger goal that seeks to create a new social and economic order.

"We work," says the Center's website, "with individuals, institutions, businesses, and communities to conserve natural resources, counter the commercialization of our culture, support community engagement, and promote positive changes in the way goods are produced and consumed."

One of the co-founders of the Center is Juliet Schor, a professor of sociology who also has a Ph.D. in economics. She called one of her books *Plenitude*. It was recently re-issued with a new title, *True Wealth*. The subtitle is: *How and Why Millions of Americans Are Creating a Time-Rich, Ecologically Light, Small-Scale, High-Satisfaction Economy.*

A mouthful, but I think it captures the essence of what it is that the Center hopes millions of Americans will help it to create. If it succeeds in doing it here, I assume it will also attempt to do it elsewhere.

Doing things that help this Center — or a similar organization — to achieve its goals is another way to help speed the move to a more sustainable lifestyle.

Fixing the perception problem

> Unless the danger from climate change is perceived to be real and [one for which] immediate action is warranted, the public is likely to reject required and costly lifestyle changes.
>
> Sheldon Kamieniecki and Michael Kraft
> *Climate Change*[8]

Perhaps the biggest challenge for our gifted storytellers is to make people aware of the eco-dangers they face, without freezing them with fear. To help them see that their way of life is triggering bad-for-us chain reactions in the natural world, that many of these are close to the runaway stage, and that some may already be in it. But at the same time to also make them aware that there is something they can do to influence the way things unfold.

Why is doing this a big challenge? Because there is a big disconnect between the sense of imminent disaster that many scientists are getting from their studies, and the low level of a sense of urgency felt by a large percentage of the public. The gap is larger in the U.S. than in other developed countries. I would guess it's as big if not bigger in fast developing countries such as China, India, and Brazil. Neither scientists nor the media seem able to close the gap.

What the science says

A team of twenty-nine scientists (including a Nobel prizewinner) recently published a paper in which they outlined their concept of "a safe operating space for humanity."[9] They identify nine of the Earth's "biophysical subsystems or processes" that together determine whether or not the planet will move out of its current Holocene state (one that happens to be exceptionally hospitable for the kind of critters we are). The nine are:

- Climate change
- Rate of biodiversity loss (terrestrial and marine)
- Interference with the nitrogen and phosphorous cycles
- Stratospheric ozone depletion
- Ocean acidification
- Global freshwater use
- Change in land use
- Chemical pollution
- Atmospheric aerosol loading

For each of these nine "processes" they tried to define boundaries or limits that, if exceeded, are likely to tip components of them, such as a monsoon system, "into a new state [with] deleterious or potentially disastrous consequences for humanity." They note that many subsystems "react in a nonlinear, often abrupt way, and are particularly sensitive around threshold levels of certain key variables."

The team's goal is to associate each boundary or threshold with a critical value for one or more control variables, such as carbon dioxide concentration. They note that the limits aren't yet well-defined in all cases. But they think we have overstepped them in three cases (seriously for climate change, more so for the N_2 half of the nitrogen-phosphorous cycles, and way out there for biodiversity loss).

And, "we may soon be approaching the boundaries for global freshwater use, change in land use, ocean acidification, and interference with the global phosphorous cycle."

These aren't the only scientists who think we have or are on the verge of setting off irreversible chain reactions in systems the earth uses to maintain our current benign Holocene state. For her book *Field Notes from a Catastrophe*, Elizabeth Kolbert visited researchers studying the effects of warming in the Arctic. They talked about the feedback loops involved in the thawing of permafrost and the disappearance of sea ice.

Permafrost holds billions of tons of partly decomposed organic material. As it thaws and its temperature rises, that material breaks down, adding carbon dioxide and methane to the atmosphere. Which creates more warming. "It's like ready-use mix," one researcher told Kolbert, "just a little heat and it will start cooking." He called it "a time bomb, just waiting for a little warmer conditions."[10]

Sea ice covered with snow reflects between eighty and ninety percent of incident sunlight, more than anything else on the planet. The ocean sends back only around seven percent, about as low as you can go. "So," said another expert, "what you're doing is replacing the best reflector with the worst ... As we melt that ice back, we can put more heat into the system, which means we can melt the ice back even more [and] you see, it just kind of builds on itself ... it takes a small nudge to the climate system and amplifies it into a big change."

What the public thinks

Do all climate scientists say they think we are at the edge of several critical thresholds? Probably not, but enough do based on what seem to be solid findings. Enough, that is, for me to feel that a cross-disciplinary chunk of our science is telling us there's reason for all of us to feel a sense of urgency. But a lot of people, especially in the U.S., seem to have not heard that message, or not heard it in a way that grabs them viscerally.

The Pew Research Center has for several years run a poll of ordinary citizens about their "Opinions about Global Warming." Here are some findings.[11]

One question asks: "How serious a problem?" In January 2007 less than half — 45% — said "very serious." Since then the world of science has continued to issue fresh warnings. But by October 2010 the percentage of folks who said that had dropped to 32%. Despite severe weather events over the next two years the number, in October 2012, was up but only to 39%, perhaps because people were more preoccupied with the state of the economy.*

These findings are echoed in Gallup's annual "environmental" polls.[12] One question: "*How much do you personally worry about global warming?*" Here are the percentages of those who say "worry a great deal":

In 2007: 53%; in 2010: 32%; and in 2012: 38%.

Oh, and if the climate is changing, does our way of life have anything to do with it? Both polls ask their versions of that question. (*Pew: If the earth is warming, is it because of human activity? Gallup: Are temperature changes due to man-made or natural causes?*) The percentages of folk who think "we done it":

Pew:	2007,47%;	2010, 34%;	2012, 45%.
Gallup:	2007, 61%;	2010, 50%;	2012, 53%.

So let's say that currently only four in ten adult Americans are seriously worried about our ecosystem, and only half see the connection between its state and how we live.

* And perhaps also because at some level people know there"s a conflict between wishing for a hotter economy and a cooler globe.

How does that compare with the percentage of scientists who say mea culpa? In a recent poll around 3,100 "earth scientists" were asked, in essence, Is the Earth warming, and if so is human activity a "significant factor."

90% of them said yes to the first question. And 82% said, yes, mea culpa. The authors of the study conclude by saying: "It seems that the debate on the authenticity of global warming and the role played by human activity is largely non-existent among those who understand the nuances and scientific basis of long-term climate processes."[13]

But the public thinks there's no such consensus among scientists. The Pew poll quoted earlier also asked: "*Do scientists agree the earth is getting warmer because of human activity?*"

In their 2006 poll, 59% said yes, 29% said no (the rest said "don't know"). In 2010, the numbers were even: 44% said yes, and 44% said no.

Frustrates the scientists. Some blame the media.

Scientific American published a story about a meeting held in February 2011 by the American Association for the Advancement of Science.[14]

Members of the media were invited to participate. Some sparks flew in the Friday morning session. Toward the end of it, Kerry Emanuel, a climate scientist from MIT, asked a panel of journalists "why the media continues to cover anthropogenic climate change as a controversy or debate" among scientists, when it is not.

"You haven't persuaded the public," Elizabeth Shogren of National Public Radio, is reported to have said.

"Emanuel immediately countered, smiling and pointing a finger at Shogren, 'No, you haven't.' " Applause from the scientists in the room.

Modify the terminology

The idea that there is no solid consensus among scientists about the existence and causes of climate change is like the smile of the Cheshire cat in the story of Alice in Wonderland. The smile persists, floats around in the air even though there is no cat.

I dwell a bit on this idea because neutralizing it may be one of the most important parts of our storytellers' task. Why would people feel there's any urgent need for us to change our ways if they believe that even our scientists don't agree that the need exists? So the idea keeps being put out there by those who want us to stay wedded to our "hyper-consumption" lifestyle. And it seems to be one that's hard for big media to squelch, even for those in it who know it isn't true.

Why? Andrew Revkin, a journalist who has written about what's happening with the environment for more than two decades, says one answer is to be found in what he calls "The Tyranny of Balance."[15]

Journalists, he says, have "long relied on the age-old method of finding a yea-sayer and a nay-sayer to frame any issue ... It is an easy way for reporters to show they have no bias. [When] this format is overused, it tends to highlight the opinions of people at the polarized edges of a debate [and] to focus attention on a handful of telegenic or quotable people working in the field who are not necessarily the greatest authorities."

The practice "has been exploited by opponents of emissions curbs [ever since] big companies whose profits were tied to fossil fuels recognized they could use [it] to amplify the inherent uncertainties in climate projections and thus [hope to delay the imposition of limits on] burning those fuels."

He has some ideas about how to minimize this kind of exploitation. One is that reporters, when they interview or quote people, make an effort to find out and to disclose any connections those folks have with groups who may have an interest in putting a spin on the story.

Yes that would help. But in any discussion of the Cheshire cat's smile there's something else journalists — and the rest of us — can do that doesn't require any effort. Quit using the term "scientific consensus" to describe where most of those folks stand on the issue. You can say a group has a consensus view if 51% of its members hold it. But 82% is not just a majority, it's one by a landslide. So call it what it is, the scientific view by a landslide. If you must use the "c" word, add an adjective to it — runaway, or huge, or overwhelming. Big or large will also do.

Revkin also says that it's hard for journalists to give the subject of global warming as much space as it deserves. Or to talk about it in a way that makes it stick in people's minds.

"The incremental nature of climate change and its uncertain scenarios [make] the issue of global warming incompatible with the news process ... Journalism craves the concrete, the known, the here and now and is repelled by conditionality, distance, and the future."

What's not "here and now" about melting ice caps, charged-up hurricanes and weird weather? Well, yes, they are concrete enough but you can't "draw a straight line" between any one of those events and an increase in the globe's overall temperature.

"Even extreme climate anomalies, such as a decade-long superdrought in the West, could never be shown to be definitively caused by human-driven warming."

There used to be a time, he says, when the big environmental issues of the day got a lot of coverage. For example, in the 1980s "the prime environmental issues [revolved] around iconic incidents that were catastrophic in nature ... Love Canal ... Bhopal ... Chernobyl ... *Exxon Valdez*." All those things had clear causes, and there were things you could do about them that didn't require big changes in the way we live. Love Canal, for example, was "quickly followed by Superfund cleanup laws."

And then there was the Ozone Hole. Again, clearly linked to our use of a group of chemicals, and soon there was an international treaty that banned them. What made it great news was that "it was an issue with an emblem — the stark, seasonal 'hole' [and] a satellite image of a giant purple bruiselike gap in the planet's radiation shield. [The] ozone hole still resonates in the popular imagination [because] it is so memorable ..."

But, he adds, "you will never see a headline in a major paper reading 'Global Warming Strikes: Crops Wither, Coasts Flood, Species Vanish.' All of those things may happen in plain sight in coming decades, but they will occur so dispersed in time and geography that they will not constitute news as we know it."

The task for our storytellers

So perhaps our storytellers need to focus on two related questions: *how to connect events that are "dispersed in time and geography,"* and *how to make them iconic, associated with one or more memorable images.*

We can find some answers by looking at how the Traditionals talk — and have been talking for decades — about what they see going on. Back in the 1970s Rolling Thunder put it this way:

> When you have pollution in one place, it spreads all over. It spreads just as arthritis or cancer spreads

> in the body. The earth is sick now because [it] is being mistreated, and some of the problems that may occur, some of the natural disasters that might happen in the near future, are only the natural readjustments that have to take place to throw off sickness.
>
> A lot of things are on this land that don't belong here. They're [like] viruses or germs. Now, we may not recognize the fact when it happens, but [this] is really going to be like fever or vomiting, what you might call physiological adjustment.[16]

He and other Native Americans call this period of adjustment the "purification."

Shortly after I emerged from my querencia I asked for and was granted an interview with R.T. It was the mid-1980s, more than a dozen years had passed since he made that statement. I asked him when he thought the period of purification would begin.

"It has started," he said. He thought it would last for forty years, perhaps more. Hard to pin things down in our time scale when you are talking about how long it takes the earth to do something.

He must have sensed my dismay. "What will happen, how bad things will be for us," he said, "is not fixed. It depends also on what we do about the situation."

What follows are some morals of the story.

Play the Ma Bio and pollution cards

> Viewed from the distance of the moon, the astonishing thing about the earth, catching the breath, is that it is alive. The photographs show the dry, pounded surface of the moon, dead as an old bone. Aloft, floating free beneath the moist, gleaming membrane of blue sky, is the rising earth, the only exuberant thing in this part of the cosmos ... It has the

> organized, self-contained look of a live creature, full of information, marvelously skilled in handing the sun.
>
> — Lewis Thomas, *The Lives of a Cell*[17]

The spring of 2011 was the wettest on record for parts of Vermont (and perhaps elsewhere). The water in Lake Champlain rose to a record height and flooded many nearby communities. The rain let up for a few days and the water level began to inch lower. Then more rain.

I went to the general store to pick up a copy of the *Burlington Free Press*. The headline on the first page said: "Worst may be yet to come." Below it was a picture of a man climbing into his kayak to navigate the flooded Main Street of his town.

The woman at the checkout counter glanced at the headline and the picture. She'd never said more than "have a good day" to me. This time she looked up from the paper and said "Mother Earth is mad."

Two few weeks later I ran into a man I'll call Earl, a general contractor who has done some work for me. The weather had continued to be drizzly with only a few breaks. "You must be backed up on your outside jobs," I said. "Way behind," he said. Pause. "We've been messing with Nature," he added, "polluted her land and waters. She's striking back, and she's a lot more powerful than we are."

Earl's never heard of Rolling Thunder, but here he was echoing his words. Made me wonder. For R.T., the earth "is a living organism, the body of [a being] who has a will and wants to be well, who is at times less [or] more healthy, physically and mentally." His being isn't vindictive, perhaps even does what she has to do with a touch of sadness. But vengeful or not, does this ancient idea that there is such a being linger not only in the Traditional world but also deep inside all of us?

It is an idea most scientists scorn as pure superstition. It's OK to think of the biosphere acting in some ways like an organism, but let's not start taking about it as if it was a real being, not even as a metaphor. Lovelock got a lot of grief for daring to use the word Gaia in conjunction with his idea that the biosphere acts to make the earth's climate suitable for it. He continues to use it but goes to great lengths to make clear it's "only a metaphor." Just kidding, folks.

But why not use the metaphor if it evokes a powerful image that grabs us viscerally, and also ties together events "dispersed in time and geography?" They are all mechanisms the earth uses to stay healthy.

"Mother Earth is mad." Four words that capture the essence of the situation. Yes, something unusual is going on, and it's in part a reaction we've provoked.

There is one other idea to be gleaned from the way Rolling Thunder and Earl talked about what's happening. Neither of them mentioned global warming. They went straight to the source of not only that but also other troublesome ecological developments: pollution.

People can argue about whether the earth really is getting hotter and, if it is, whether that is due to some natural causes. It's harder to deny that there's mercury and PCBs in our fish, and pesticides in our meat and potatoes and sides of spinach. And harder to argue that sunspots poured those and other poisons into our biosphere.

So perhaps pollution can be the lead-in to or even the central theme of the stories we tell to make people aware that there's an urgent need to change our way of life. Because it is triggering chain reactions in the earth's natural systems and processes, some of which are close to becoming or already are in a runaway stage.

Taking on the "ads"

> [Studies] show that beyond a certain level, increasing consumption does not correlate with increasing happiness. In fact, the percentage of Americans who describe themselves as 'very happy' peaked in 1957 and has remained stable or declined ever since.
>
> — Kaufman and Franz[18]

How can we speed a shift away from a way of life that is headed for ecological bankruptcy? Another way is to loosen the hold of one of the things that keep us chained to it.

Our "culture of consumption," say Kaufman and Franz, "is fueled by advertising — the art of making wants appear to be needs. The basic premise [is] that we can never have enough: advertising succeeds when it convinces us that we are not satisfied with what we already have." Doing this is very big business. "In 2002, global spending on advertising climbed to $446 billion, about nine times the amount spent in 1950."

The art also has a craft side. One major tool is "market research" — pinpointing who is the target of any given ad, what that "consumer's" fears, aspirations, and other ego needs are, what kind of product name and packaging is most likely to grab that set of folks viscerally.

Another tool is studies that help companies to develop "products designed to wear out, break down, to become dated." Hey, the cool people have moved on, not too late to join them.

These two things — clever ads and making things seem outmoded — have "fueled consumer desire." But it was the credit card that "allowed the average citizen to act on impulse."

Ads fuel our desire for a high-consumption lifestyle by equating it with happiness and by making it a yardstick for success. They are aided in this enterprise by powerful political and economic forces. But recent events have shown us that powerful regimes can be overthrown by those they rule, and that this can happen quickly.

The rulers in this case are not the makers of either the ads or of the goods and services they tout. They are only trying to make a living like the rest of us. The rulers are ultimately our own wishes to appear hip and successful.

Earlier, I mentioned what others are doing in the fight against ads that prey on these wishes. (Those others included, you may recall, the various voluntary simplicity movements and organizations such as the *Center for a New American Dream.*) Here's something else that, if done, could both help those folks in their battles and become a new front in the war.

Imagine a consumer uprising, instigated and sustained by a growing network of folks who use both new and old media to tell different stories about how to look cool and be smart. For example, by:

- Not borrowing to buy anything that is not an absolute necessity.
- Not buying things that could be made to last a lot longer than they do.
- Spreading the news when "it's new" doesn't mean it's better.
- Demanding goods that can be made, repaired, upgraded, and recycled locally.

If we do something like this we can help blunt the impact of ads that fuel mindless consumption. Those who want to encourage our current buying habits have very big budgets, but we the consumers are the majority owners of the modern economy. That gives us a lot of power to influence its direction, if enough of us decide to do it. And if we keep at it for as long as is needed to get results.

It's unlikely to be a short fight. What can help to keep us going are creative ways to celebrate our interim wins, both little and big.

Tackling the mastodon in the room

> [Democracy] cannot survive overpopulation. Human dignity cannot survive it. Convenience and decency cannot survive it. As you put more and more people in the world, the value of life not only declines, it disappears ... The more people there are, the less one individual matters.
>
> — Isaac Asimov
> science and science fiction writer

Most articles, books, and talk shows about how to live sustainably focus on technology — more efficient solar cells or windmills or mini nuclear power plants. Or gene modification to increase crop and herd yields. Some also talk about things each of us can do to conserve energy and produce less waste. But almost none say anything about what might be done about the mastodon in the room: seven billion people on the planet, a number projected to reach nine billion by mid-century.

The math is not complicated. Our total consumption of natural resources equals the average amount used up per person times the number of people. Thus far we've talked about reducing the rate at which we are depleting those resources by shifting to a less "hyper-consumption" lifestyle. But that won't lower the rate by a lot if we keep adding more people to the equation. Wouldn't it help a lot if we could look forward to two billion *fewer* people by mid-century?

There are people — the "cornucopians" — who believe that "a growing population can actually help [us] to become more prosperous, since [it means] both more consumers and more producers."[10] But what if in the process we deplete the planet's capacity to support us, or even push it out of its hospitable (to us) Holocene state? Not to worry, because we humans are the ultimate resource. "Human inventiveness will solve any problems — environmental, economic, social, or otherwise — that may beset continued population growth."[19]

Sounds to me like magical thinking, the kind that leads to dreams of making perpetual motion machines. And another group of people who, like the wolf haters, need to be "outshouted, out-financed, and outvoted."

But what about all the people — many more, I hope — who don't think that way? Why aren't they talking a lot more than they are about how to slow down our rate of population growth or even reverse that trend? The zero-population-growth movement seems to have stalled. For sure it hasn't kept our numbers from growing exponentially. Why doesn't a part of every discussion about a sustainable future focus on what such failures can teach us about more effective ways of attaining that goal?

Perhaps because the problem seems so intractable that people have lost hope of finding fresh and more viable solutions for it. So why waste time talking about it. I could understand, even accept that view, if the solution depended on some impossible to surmount technology hurdles. But, as the writer Garrett Hardin reminds us, that's not so.

"As a scientist I wanted to find a scientific solution; but reason inexorably led me to conclude that the population problem could not possibly be solved without repudiating certain ethical beliefs and altering some of the political and economic arrangements of contemporary society."

So we are back to the common ground in which the causes of our eco-problems are rooted: our "attitudes, values, and beliefs." And back to my reason for thinking this fight can also be won if our storytellers, our modern world's equivalents of traditional healers, work to align our internal landscape with our natural world's sacred order.

Unlike the challenges for our storytellers that I've outlined thus far, I have no ideas about how they might set about changing the "ethical beliefs and [the] political and economical arrangements" that keep fattening the mastodon.

All I can do is to remind them that our history is full of examples of how what seemed like an "impossible" task for one generation proved to be doable for the next. And to leave them with a list of quotes that have been around for a while — none may be new to you or to them. But perhaps glancing at them again will evoke some images or thoughts that can be woven into one or more healing stories.

The list

The following are quotes I selected from a posting by "Vermonters for a Sustainable Population."[20] I didn't check the sources for accuracy, but was assured by VSP staff that they had done that.

Here's the short list:

- "The Great Challenge: Can you think of any problem in any area of human endeavor on any scale from microscopic to global, whose long-term solution is in any demonstrable way aided, assisted, or advanced by further increases in population locally, nationally, or globally?"

  A. Bartlett, Professor Emeritus of Physics,
  University of Colorado, Boulder

- "You never know what is enough until you know what is more than enough."

  William Blake, poet and artist

- "Should conservationists find the wisdom and courage to come back to calling for population stabilization, we must stress how the population explosion causes the ecological wounds that result in mass extinction and destruction of the biosphere."

  David Foreman, Founder of Earth First!
  and head of Rewilding Institute

- "No decision any of us makes will have more effect on the world (and on our lives) than whether to bear another child. No decision then should be made with more care."

  Bill McKibben, author and
  scholar-in-residence at Middlebury College

- "You know, I have often thought that at the end of the day, we would have saved more wildlife if we had spent all WWF's money on buying condoms."

  Sir Peter Scott, founder of the World Wildlife Fund

- "[It has been said] that human population growth within the ecosystem was closely analogous to the growth of malignant tumor cells within an organism, that man was acting like a cancer on the biosphere. The multiplication of human numbers certainly seems wild and uncontrolled ... We seem to be doing all right at the moment; but if you could ask cancer cells, I suspect they would think they were doing fine. But when the organism dies, so do they; and for our own, selfish, practical, utilitarian reasons, I think we should be careful about how we influence the rest of the ecosystem."

  Marston Bates, American zoologist and writer

- "Mankind is looking for food not just on this planet but on others. Perhaps the time has now come to put that process into reverse, Instead of controlling the environment for the benefit of the population, maybe we should control the population to ensure the survival of our environment."

  Sir David Attenborough, author and contributor to TV documentaries

- "Basically, then, there are only two kinds of solutions to the population problem. One is a 'birth control solution,' in which we find ways to lower the birth rate. The other is a 'death rate solution.' in which ways to raise the death rate — war, famine, pestilence — find us."

  Paul Ehrlich, author of *The Population Bomb*

- "We have looked for, and have not found, any convincing argument for continued population growth. The health of our economy does not depend on it, nor does the vitality of business, nor the welfare of the average person."

  John D. Rockefeller III, then-Chair, Commission on Population and the American Future

12

Reasons for hope

> **Saving grace**, a quality that makes up for other generally negative characteristics: *He was a born misfit whose saving grace was his boundless generosity.*
>
> — *The Random House Dictionary* (an unabridged edition)

There are already storytellers out there whose books and songs and movies, whether or not designed to do it, promote alignment with the "sacred" order of the natural world. I hope this book will add to their number. But even if it is a big addition, will their efforts make any difference? Will they create enough of a change in our stance toward the natural world and thereby accelerate our shift to a more sustainable way of life?

The mind shift needed is from one that equates our success as a species with our ability to dominate and exploit the natural world, to one that sees that our survival depends on being able to cooperate with and be guided by it. Yes, there is a growing number of people who have made this shift but not enough to force major changes in public and business policies. What we need to do is to accelerate the pace at which those numbers grow.

Whether the ideas our storytellers float out there will do this depends in part on the nature of the ground on which those seeds fall. The following are some of the things about it that I find encouraging.

Our creativity

The outward manifestation of our creativity is the ability to invent clever new tools or ways to express our ideas and emotions. The move to a less "hyper-consumption" lifestyle will of course require a lot of this kind of innovation. I have no doubt that we can do this, given a sufficient sense of the precariousness of our situation. But this is not the only aspect of our creativity that gives me reason to be hopeful about our future.

I've been in the "creative problem-solving" business for over twenty-five years. I've helped a lot of people to develop fresh ideas for solving both personal and business problems. Often an idea that gets the problem "owners" past a conceptual block is new only to them, not to the world. In such cases can the process that got them there be called creative? No, if measured by the Patent Office's requirement of originality. But perhaps yes if to get the idea they had to transcend a piece of their conditioning.

What keeps us from seeing a new aspect of something is our old, habitual way of looking at it. We see the world most of the time as we were taught to see it, whether by specific people or by our milieu. But we have the ability to shake free of those habits of thought. The result can be a tiny aha that does something for only one person. Or it can be one that changes the way our next few generations think about something. Like Newton's flash of insight.

Here's the physicist David Bohm's take on what happened in Newton's head. At the time, no one asked why the moon stayed up in the sky. Why didn't it fall to the earth? No need to ask, because the answer was obvious: Heavenly and earthly matters don't behave the same way.

People and pebbles fall, the moon doesn't. "It's celestial matter, it stays up where it belongs."[1]

"That explanation," Bohm adds, "may have made sense in ancient times, [but by] the time of Newton [there] was evidence [that the two kinds of] matter were [not] all that different." But no one questioned the explanation because "there was an old habit in the mind to not question it — just take it for granted."

Bohm speculates that the question did nag Newton. When he saw the apple falling, "it may have been in his mind: 'why isn't the moon falling?' And he suddenly had the answer: 'The moon *is* falling. That's the force of universal gravitation. Everything is falling towards every thing.'"

But the moon doesn't reach the ground because some of those forces are also making it fall outward. The net result is to make it move in an orbit around the earth.

"The key point of the insight," Bohm adds, "was to break the old habit of thought." After that "it was not very difficult" for Newton to go on to develop his laws of motion.

Creativity, fundamentally, is the ability to transcend our conditioning. After my many years in the business I'm convinced that it is part of our genetic inheritance. This is not to say that we are all equally creative in all areas. We've also inherited the ability to run on two legs, but not all of us can run a sub four-minute mile or set an Olympic long-jump record.

But it seems reasonable to assume that when it's a question of shaking free of ideas that threaten our collective survival, natural selection would have worked to give enough of us the ability to see something — that what we were taught to believe was a winning way of life is not sustainable. Even though that "habit of thought" has been around for thousands of years.

The capacity for caring

> It is no time to be afraid — [only] time to think of the future, and to challenge the destruction of your grandchildren, and to move away from the four-year cycle of living [from] one election to another, and think about the coming generations.
>
> — Oren Lyons, Iroquois (Six Nations) Chief[2]

Let's say our storytellers succeed in making a lot of people see that there's an urgent need to change the way we live. That it's not only some of our scientists who are telling us we may be on the verge of flipping the earth out of its current nice-for-us Holocene state, but that the earth seems to be saying the same thing.

Assume further that they also get people thinking: Hey, perhaps this won't happen in our lifetime, but if the odds are even one in five of it happening in that of our grandchildren it behooves us to start making those changes now. A worthy intent, but what happens when they see that doing it in any significant way will mean making sacrifices?

Breaking free of any regime or regimen is a struggle. This one is both — a regime we put in place ourselves, and an addictive regimen. The struggle is likely to be epic, perhaps more difficult than any we've won against colonial powers or homebred dictators. And one that may last for more than one generation.

Because the struggle is against not only those of our kin who have a vested interest in hanging on to the current order, but our own desires — such as for a life of push-button ease, a strong stock market, and the reluctance to declare Nature the ultimate winner in the war we've waged on it.

The sacrifices will include those imposed by voluntary austerity, such as loss of conveniences and ways of having fun; those that accompany periods of major change, such as loss of stability and the sense of security that comes with it; and perhaps broken heads — no matter how peaceful the struggle, it could trigger a violent response from those who feel threatened by it.

Do we have the stomach for it? OK, the cause — a better future for our children — has always been a big motivator. But the greater concern here is not for the children of today whom we can see and touch, but for the imagined ones who might be their children or those children's grandchildren. Are our feelings for them strong enough to make us act on their behalf?

What we need to do is, in essence, to engage in a sustained act of altruism, which my dictionary says is "the principle or practice of unselfish concern for or devotion to the welfare of others," in this case, that of the children to come.

OK, we all know or know of people who act in selfless ways, who willingly give to others their time, their money, even their lives. But it's the me-firsters who seem to rule our world. So is selfishness the essence of our nature and altruism a thin veneer we spray onto it to make us seem other than what we are? I think not. Here's why.

There is now a piece of technology that enables neuroscientists to probe the workings of our brains without pushing wires into them, or subjecting them to the risks of CT or PET scans (x-rays, or the introduction of "radionuclide" tracers, or both).* The less invasive technique is called "functional magnetic resonance imaging," or fMRI. It allows you to see the neural networks that are activated in the brain when you do things, including both physical and mental tasks. (Conventional MRIs create pictures of the anatomy of the brain, not images of it at work.)

* CT: X-ray Computed Tomography; PET: Positron Emission Tomography.

Increasingly, neuroscientists have been using the technology to study parts of the brain that seem to be involved in making moral decisions. One study that focused on acts of altruism was done a few years ago by a team of six neuroscientists. It was funded in part by the U.S. National Institutes of Health. They published their findings in a paper titled "*Human fronto-mesolimbic networks guide decisions about charitable donation*."[3]

The paper is written in the flat, affect-free tone scientists use when they write for their peers. Lots of details about "materials and methods," the results described in a way that makes it hard for a lay reader to separate the bits that only confirm or elaborate on what's already known from those that provide a fresh insight.

Thankfully, the authors also published, in a different forum, a brief one-paragraph description of their findings. It was titled "*Neural Basis of Human Altruism*."[4] The first sentence says:

"This was the first study to show that altruistic decisions — such as donating money to charity — lead to activation of the mesolimbic pathway, the primary reward system of the brain."

This and the rest of the paragraph confirmed what I had thought were the new bits in the original paper, as well as my understanding of some of the other things that were said in it.

The mesolimbic pathway "rewards" an act by releasing chemicals that make you feel good. The authors note that this system "regulates overall reward reinforcement [and] is activated by a host of stimuli, including food, sex, drugs, and money." It seems we're turned on not only by those things but also acts of altruism. A *Washington Post* story about the study said its findings suggest that altruism was "not a superior moral faculty that suppresses basic selfish urges but rather was basic to the brain, hard-wired and pleasurable."[5]

There's more. The study found that making charitable donations to a cause also activated a second reward system whose circuits don't light up when you make money. This system is located in the "subgenual" area of the brain, and "plays key roles in social attachments [in] humans and other animals." The authors note that this "subgenual cortex and adjacent septal structures [were also activated] when humans looked at their own babies and romantic partners."

Making money gives us a kick. Altruism on behalf of our kids may give us a kick and a half.

So perhaps we do have what it takes to make a long-term commitment to the goal of bequeathing a sustainable way of life to our now and future children. At least our neural circuits seem designed to help us do it, to provide compensation for the sacrifices the doing will require us to make.

The gut connection

> It is my conviction that there is within the human individual a sense, whether at a conscious or unconscious level, of *relatedness to [the] nonhuman environment*, that this relatedness is one of the transcendentally important facts of human living ... if [we] try to ignore its importance [we do] so at peril to [our] psychological wellbeing.
>
> — Harold F. Searles, M.D.
> *The Nonhuman Environment*[6]

If, as noted earlier, our wellbeing and ultimately our survival depend on the health of our ecosystem, then it's likely that concern for it would, over time, become embedded in our nature. How might that concern manifest itself?

In my case it was falling into a deep depression with nothing in my personal circumstances to justify it. Thinking back, it's clear that I suffered from a milder and more easily ignored version of it for several years before I fell into that pit.

I think I see signs of that eco-despair in other people, many of who seem not to be aware of the source of their unease. And the numbers of those who exhibit these symptoms seems to have increased a lot in the last dozen or so years. Especially among our teenagers.

I could of course be imagining an epidemic that isn't out there. OK, so perhaps there is a real increase in the number of people who seem to be depressed, whether mildly or more severely. But there may be other causes for that outbreak.

One could be the pace at which the modern world requires us to live. It's possible that it is out of sync with the slower rhythms and cycles that our bodies and psyches inherited from the more than million years of our history. Another cause could be the speed at which our technical inventions push us to change the way we do things. Again, more quickly than we may be designed to handle without getting stressed out. And then there are the chemicals we've put into the air we breathe, the food we eat, and the water we drink. Could they be acting as downers?

It wouldn't be hard to add more items to the list. So it's possible that eco-despair is not nearly as widespread as I imagine it to be, that what I see in others' unease is a reflection of my version of it, not theirs.

Perhaps, and perhaps not. It seems I'm not the only one who thinks that an increasing number of our psychic ills may have something to do with our links to the natural world. There are now books and articles out there about "ecopsycholology" and "ecotherapy." Their thesis is, in essence, that we are emotionally connected to nature and that we are troubled by the extent to which modern life has severed that connection. The fix is to get back in touch with it. Hug a tree or spend some time in one of our National Parks.

This is not quite what I'm saying. The malaise I'm talking about is not the one created by distance from the natural world. You could be living in an Alaskan wilderness and still feel it because the health of your psyche is linked to that of the biosphere. When it becomes sick, so do we.

If I'm right about this, there is a growing segment of people who have caught a case of eco-despair. That's good news for our storytellers. It increases the odds that the ideas they float out there will find soil in which they can root and grow.

13

What I choose to believe

> In the old physics, matter (which was the only reality) was completely mechanical, leaving no room for mind. But if, according to the new physics, everything is enfolded in everything else, then there is no real separation of domains. Mind grows out of matter. And matter contains the essence of mind.
>
> Quantum physicist David Bohm[a]

In the last three chapters I've talked about a way forward that gives me hope that we can shift our stance toward the natural world. It's what I think we need to do to both find a sustainable way of life and to soften the blow of the eco-disasters we've already set in motion.

In the lead-in to those chapters I also mentioned a more far-out possibility: that these efforts to increase our alignment with nature's ""sacred"" order might incline forces associated with it to give us some assists. But I didn't say more about what those forces might be or what makes me think they exist. That was because the alignment task is something I feel needs to be done anyway. Neither our storytellers nor anyone else they enlist needs to accept the idea that the impact of what they do might be amplified by some other-than-human mover. If that is something that can happen, it will happen anyway.

So why do I need to say anything more about what that "mover" could be? I've already talked about forces and powers — including Eddington's "Universal Mind or Logos" (back in chapter 5) — that were candidates for inclusion in my version of James's unseen order. You also know that I chose to look for some in Native American ideas about that invisible world, and you may be familiar with those concepts. But I didn't say much about which, if any, of these ideas met my inclusion criteria. These were, you may recall, that the existence of a principle or entity was something that:

- Didn't violate any of the laws of physics or chemistry or biology that I knew about.
- Was one for which I could imagine how it could have arisen and might operate — explanations that seemed reasonable to me, even if they existed only in my head.
- Was consistent with my experiences and intuitions.

My reason for describing some candidates but not saying which met these criteria was to avoid leaving you with the feeling that I was trying to get you to buy them. That's not a business I want to be in. So I hoped putting the ideas out there would be enough to help you decide for yourself which of them did or not seem plausible to you, by the above or any other criteria. And so you would be creating, as we went along, a picture of your own unseen order.

Again, please keep in mind that the way forward I've described in the preceding chapters does not require adoption of any part of my conception of that order.

Aspects of my unseen order

What follows is a description of the main ideas that I've chosen to make a part of my unseen order. As such, they reflect what I believe the nature of things to be. The word "belief" can suggest conviction or certainty. Neither is what I mean to imply here when I say that "I believe" something. Those words are shorthand for: "I think the idea that it exists or is true seems plausible enough to become a provisional element of my picture of reality."

As noted earlier, an unseen power can be conceived of as an "abstract ideality" or as a Being "*in concreto*." The former sits at what William James might call the Emersonian end of a spectrum, the latter at the end preferred by James. Some of the powers and forces that inhabit my unseen order could be situated at either end, and I'll talk about them first.

The animate earth

> Some striking concepts emerge when we accept the idea that the biosphere is the fundamental unit of Earthlife. The history of Earthlife then becomes the tale of the continuous survival and evolution of the biosphere from its origin on the prebiotic Earth ... One reason the [idea of] the biosphere as [a] unit of life may seem strange to us is that [its] metabolism [takes] place on a time scale of thousands or millions of years, a very long time in human terms ...
>
> — Gerald Feinberg and Robert Shapiro
> *Life Beyond Earth*[1]

Is the notion that the earth, or at least its biosphere, is a living organism more than a metaphor? Yes, say the authors of *Life Beyond Earth*, and I find their argument persuasive.

The writers (also quoted earlier) are, you may recall, Robert Shapiro, a chemist, and Gerald Feinberg, a physicist (both with impressive credentials). They wrote the book because they think our efforts to look for signs of extraterrestrial life are seriously blinkered. We would have a better chance of finding those signs if we defined life in a less parochial way — something that need not be carbon based and that could thrive without our kind of atmosphere and its range of temperatures.

So what's a definition of life that would apply not only to all forms of Earthlife but also others that could inhabit realms "such as the surface of boiling and frigid planets, the interiors of stars, and the clouds of isolated molecules in interstellar space"?

Feinberg and Shapiro suggest that "the vital activity of life that distinguishes it from non-life is the preservation and gradual increase of [its] internal order." Living things, in other words, are ones that find ways to neutralize the power of the universal force that pushes all matter to move, continuously, from a more- to a less-ordered state of being.

It's true that the difference is qualitative. The growth of salt crystals in a sun-heated pool of saltwater is an example of a system in which order increases.

So "living things do not differ in kind from some of their non-living analogues, [but in] the extent to which they [create and preserve] order." But here on earth "this qualitative difference is so marked as to [give rise to] a gross dissimilarity in behavior between living and non-living [things]."

Now our biosphere is "a highly ordered system of matter and energy characterized by complex cycles that maintain or gradually increase the order of the system through an exchange of energy with the environment." It is also "the largest interdependent unit" of life on earth in which "various organisms [are] interlocked with one another in elaborate [exchanges] of matter and energy, just as our own cells are combined into a larger organism.

"We might even think of the whole Earthly biosphere as a living being, composed of innumerable separate organisms as well as some parts temporarily removed from the process of active life, such as the oxygen in the environment."

But whether or not we choose to think of our biosphere as an organism that is alive, the authors add, the existence of some kind of biosphere is one of the first things for which our space probes should look. Because no smaller living things can evolve, here or elsewhere, without a biosphere in which they can be born and survive.

It's both comforting and sobering to think of our biosphere as the fundamental unit of life on earth. Comforting if you care deeply about it and see that, though we have wounded it badly, it will continue to survive and evolve. Sobering also to see how little it might matter to it whether or not we hang around. It has already seen a lot of other kinds of critters come and go in previous phases of its life.

The organism's health maintenance team

> In an ecosystem that is in [dynamic] equilibrium organisms balance each other's inputs and outputs. The long-term average of the population of each species remains at a level that the environment can support, and nutrients are continuously recycled by biogeochemical processes. As energy flows and materials cycle through the ecosystem in countless ways, equilibrium is maintained by many checks and balances.
>
> — Kaufman and Franz, *The Biosphere*

I've come to believe that there are forces and mechanisms that work to maintain the health of the "unit of life" that is our biosphere. What's a measure of health for such an entity?

"Change and response to change are characteristic of all living systems," note Kaufman and Franz, "from the individual all the way up to the biosphere."[2]

At the species level the response manifests as changes in the makeup of successive generations. For ecosystems and for the collection of them that is the biosphere, it manifests as changes in their composition, as individual species come and go. Over time, periods long by our reckoning ecosystems are, in this sense dynamic.

But if you slow down the movie, you see that ecosystems

> . . . also possess equilibrium, a condition of balance or stability. A new generation of individuals in any species is not vastly different from the previous one. [While] fire pushes back succession in one community, succession advances somewhere else, creating an overall balance of community types within the ecosystem. [It responds] to changing conditions in ways that tend to preserve an overall pattern of plant, animal, and microbial life.
>
> This property of constant adjustment to change, maintaining an overall balance is called dynamic equilibrium.

So an overall measure of the health of the biosphere is its ability to maintain this dynamic balance in each phase of its life. That requires the proper functioning of the various species that are the equivalent of its body's cells. What does it mean for things to function "properly" at that level?

Every cell in our bodies, and every one of the many creatures that live in those cells, feeds on a part of its environment and also provides food for it. The health and ultimate survival of every critter at every level depends on the right balance of give and take in these transactions. If its kind takes too little, it weakens and dies. If it takes too much its local ecosystem sickens and so eventually does the critter's tribe. And the health of the biosphere is a reflection of the overall state of wellness of all these ecosystems.

Given that the survival of every critter depends on the collective ability of its kind to "balance its inputs and outputs," it would be surprising if the urge to do that didn't get encrypted it its DNA by natural selection. Now "taking too much" usually manifests itself as growth in numbers of a species beyond the "carrying capacity" of its environment.

This can happen, but "No population of organisms increases without limit," says Rudy Boonstra, a professor of zoology at the University of Toronto. "The central question in population ecology is what regulates their numbers."

There are of course external factors such as the presence of "predators," droughts, disease, and the availability of nutrients and space. But, says Boonstra, "the answer often [is] the actions of the populations themselves." The conclusion is based in part on a study he and a colleague, Tim Karels, conducted of ground squirrels in a Canadian boreal forest.[3]

"Animals can change their reproductive output depending on certain environmental conditions," says Karels, "and one of [those] is population density." The authors increased densities in control areas by providing extra food or fencing out predators. They then removed that greater-than-normal level of food and protection. What they saw, Karels said, was that "At very high population densities, female ground squirrels basically shut down their reproduction."[4]

A response that says, in effect, don't try to take more from the environment than it can afford to give. But if both external factors and built-in injunctions act to balance an organism's "inputs and outputs," why is there a need for any other kind of force or mechanism to enter the picture? I can see at least two reasons.

The first is that there may be enough wiggle room in the laws of natural selection for species to emerge that are not restrained by those factors and undermine their ecosystem's ability to maintain its dynamic equilibrium. We are clearly an example of such a critter, and there may be or have been other less obvious ones.

Given the concept, mentioned earlier, of "the continuous survival and evolution of the biosphere from its origins on the prebiotic earth," it seems likely that forces and mechanisms would have emerged that act like its immune system. We humans have seriously compromised the biosphere's ability to stay healthy. So one task for its health maintenance team is to produce the equivalent of serums that modify our behavior or, if that's not possible, to set in motion events that make us join the dodos and the dinosaurs. This is the process that Rolling Thunder and other Traditionals think has already begun and refer to as the "purification," though they also believe that it's not too late for us to avert the worst-case scenario.

The biosphere may also have another reason to need this SWAT team, regardless of whether or not a species such as Homo Sap. is part of the equation. This is that the internal and external constraints on behavior of a species that evolve over time are likely to be ones that elicit appropriate responses to local conditions.

But there may be times when they also need to respond to something that happens elsewhere, perhaps at the other end of the globe. Such as a fire or drought that "pushes back succession in one community," requiring another to speed things up to maintain "an overall balance of community types" in the biosphere.

And I can imagine how an external force could induce a community of plants or animals to respond to nonlocal events. The mechanism could be something like the one the physicist David Bohm proposed for how a quantum wave can move a particle to respond to something that happens far away. Not by physically pushing or pulling it, but by informing it.

To "inform," he says, also means to "form from within." His scheme, he says, is analogous to the way a radar signal guides a ship on automatic pilot. The energy required to make course changes comes from the ship's engines, not the radar waves. Ditto for the radio signal that becomes the music you hear coming out of your receiver. The power needed to move its speakers comes from its battery or wall plug.

Are there forces or powers that work in something like these ways to maintain the health of the biosphere? No way to be sure, but they are a part of my unseen order.

Yes, but. Accepting the notion that the biosphere is a living organism and that there are forces that work to maintain its health leaves me sitting in Emersonian space. Mother Earth can exist as an "abstract ideality" and not a "superhuman person."

That's not where the Traditionals choose to sit. For them the Earth is a living being with a mind, as is the Sun and the Great Spirit. To what extent am I able to join them? Not as fully or as often as I would like to be there, but I am slowly getting better at doing it.

The idea that there can be a mind associated with a planet, its sun, and some larger chunk of the universe doesn't seem too far-fetched to me. It's not one that can be derived from the laws of physics or chemistry or biology. But it's also one that can't be absolutely ruled out by those laws.

That was the assurance I got, back in chapter 5, from some of the founders of the new physics. It was enough to move me to the Emersonian end of belief space, but not to its other side. To get there I needed to do two more things: imagine how something like a Universal Mind could have arisen, and then find a reason to make that possibility part of my everyday reality.

What came first, mind or matter?

In his book *Ever Since Darwin*, Stephen Jay Gould suggests that Darwin's "uncompromisingly mechanical" views banished God from the scene for any who saw the truth in his theory of evolution. Why?

Because it undermined the old "argument from design," which is "the belief that God's benevolence (indeed his very existence) can be inferred from the perfection of organic structure." A structure of such complexity and beauty could not have been created without the guiding hand of a Designer.[5]

Darwin, says Gould, "accepted the idea of excellent design but proposed a natural explanation that could not have been more contrary" to that argument. "Darwin developed an evolutionary theory based on chance variation and natural selection imposed by an external environment: a rigidly materialistic (and basically atheistic) version of evolution."

But I don't see how Darwin's "rigidly materialistic" conception is inherently atheistic, as Gould seems to assume it to be. It is so only if you insist on defining God in a certain way: a Being that created the Universe, both in the sense of causing it to come into existence, and that of working out every detail of the design of everything in it, from quarks to quasars.

I have no argument with the notion that everything evolved out of matter according to the mindless laws of our sciences. But those laws don't exclude the development we call mind. Matter gave birth to ours. Why couldn't a more Universal Mind have also evolved out of it? A Being that didn't create the universe of matter, but was created by it. Maybe in the beginning there was only the Big Bang. Then, perhaps much later, there was Mind.

And maybe not just the One, but also others associated with more regional clusters of matter. What, other than ego, could be a reason to believe that mind can be the property only of the kinds of clumps of matter that constitute earthlife?

The limits of thought

> [Each of us] participates in an inseparable way in society and in the planet as a whole. What may be suggested further is that such participation goes on to a greater collective mind, and perhaps ultimately some yet more comprehensive mind [indefinitely beyond that of] the human species as a whole.
>
> — David Bohm and B.J. Hiley[6]

David Bohm's book *The Undivided Universe* was published a year after he died. In the preface his colleague and co-author B.J. Hiley says that he hopes the book

> will be a fitting testimony to this very radical and original thinker who rejected the view of conventional quantum mechanics [because] it did not provide a coherent overall view of nature, a feature that David felt was an essential ingredient of any physical theory.

Bohm's "causal interpretation" of quantum theory fixed that problem. It also helped clean up aspects of the old theory that Hiley calls "obscure and confused." And it gave Bohm a way of thinking about the physical and mental sides of reality "which does not divide mind from matter, the observer from the observed, the subject from the object."[7]

Here are some other things Bohm says about the relationship between mind and matter.

> I look at the process of evolution as the unfoldment of the potential of matter, which at bottom becomes indistinguishable from the potential of mind …
>
> This is not to say that I equate mind with matter, or reduce the one to the other. They are, rather, two parallel streams of development which arise from a common ground. [(a)*]

* (a): D. Bohm and R. Weber dialogue, *ReVision* 1 (1978), 24–51.

What is that common ground? Bohm says that "the present state of theoretical physics" implies that what we think of as empty space is in fact filled with energy. A vast amount of it, "immensely beyond the total energy of all the known matter in the universe," all of which is "merely a ripple [in this] tremendous ocean of energy."(b) This ocean is the realm of Bohm's "implicate order" out of which both matter and mind arise or "unfold."

> Matter is related to what we pick up with our senses and perceive as relatively stable [and] subject to certain kinds of laws. Mind is more subtle, but we do not have any knowledge of mind without matter, or matter disassociated from mind or life.
>
> For example, in a growing seed almost all the matter and energy come from the environment. The seed [provides that inanimate matter] with new information that leads it to produce the living plant or animal. Who is to say then that life was not immanent [in the matter] even before the seed was planted?
>
> In the same way, [the intelligence displayed by the animal] must also be immanent in the matter that constitutes the animal. If the immanence is pursued more and more deeply in matter, I believe we eventually reach the stream which we also experience as mind, so that mind and matter fuse.
>
> We call the ultimate heights of mind transcendence; we find in the depths of matter the immanence of the whole of that which is. Both are needed, and [I think any] mysticism which would devalue cosmic consciousness and hold only to the transcendental experience is absurd.(a)

So Bohm's equations seem to suggest to him that mind is inherent in matter. Do they also provide a basis for asserting the existence of a cosmic consciousness?

No, he would say, because neither his equations nor any

(b): D. Bohm and R. Weber dialogue, *ReVision* 4 (Spring 1981), 21–74.

other product of thought can do that. This, in essence, was the answer he gave to the philosopher Renée Weber when she asked him a similar question in one of their dialogues about his quantum theory and its implications. Here's the exchange that occurred at a point in one of them.

Suppose, she says, that your ideas about how all things emerge from the energy ocean's "implicit order" are validated, will that "also entail confirmation of a universal intelligence?"

"No," says, Bohm, "it doesn't confirm it. The implicate order is still matter, and it would still be possible to regard it, if you stopped there, as [a] sort of more subtle form of mechanism."

By "stopping there" Bohm means going no further than thought and reasoning can take you. He has also said earlier that insight can take you beyond that point.

OK, says Weber, so let's not stop there. Can't insight confirm the presence of something beyond mechanism?

"But you see," Bohm says, "there is danger here. I think that it's necessary to be very disciplined or austere or whatever you want to call it, because thought can very easily, if there is not actual insight present, postulate [it], then in the next moment you will say mistakenly that [you've apprehended something].

"You see, the temptation to project has to be understood; we have to be very careful about that, [otherwise] this could become a trap."

All that can be said, he adds, is that his theory "is consistent with the notion that there's [an] actuality, a being beyond what can be grasped in thought, and that is intelligence [of the whole]."(b)

What I heard him saying to me was: "Quit looking to me, or anyone else, for assurance that such an intelligence exists. Do, if you can, the work needed to clear your screen of perception, or simply choose to believe it's out there."

Going all the way

Thought may not be able to assure me of the existence of any invisible intelligences, but it can give me reasons to live my life as if they existed.

Recall that William James had told me, in essence, that it doesn't matter whether or not some such beings actually exist. What's important is how choosing to believe that they are out there informs the way you live. So ask, he had said, what does making that choice do for you and your world? What, in this sense, is its "cash value"?

I chose to adopt elements of the worldview of the Traditionals because I found in it a compass that helps me to find what feel like the right ways to deal with everyday problems. Right in the sense that they seem to be at least partly aligned with the forces that seek to promote the health of the whole.

The compass consists of a set of principles or themes that I found in both my readings about and encounters with Native Americans. What's described below are the few I turn to most often. The meanings I ascribe to them may include misunderstandings or distortions of the originals, but they are interpretations that work for me. The themes are:

Relatedness. There are at least two intertwined ideas here. David Bohm would have embraced the first one. It entails a way of looking at the world that sees everything in it as connected, not as isolated separate bits.

The second concept has to do with our place in that world. We are in some ways unique, but not any more important than the bears or the badgers or the pinyon trees.

Our right to be here is not greater than theirs. In many ways they are wiser than we are. They are relatives, in more than the metaphorical sense of the word.

Reciprocity. Something I've touched on before several times. The idea is that taking something from your world obliges you to give something back to it, to not break the circle of giving.

Responsibility. My take on this one has to do with one of the ways in which we humans are unique. Our brains enable us to act in ways that are ultimately self-defeating. We are smart enough to see that something we do is destructive in that sense, but also clever enough to fool ourselves into thinking that it isn't so. That gives us enormous power to do harm to others and to ourselves. So it behooves us to use that power with great care and restraint. And I in my life need to strive to do that whether or not I see us doing it collectively.

Appropriateness. I found that to determine what is suitable or fit for an occasion or purpose the Traditionals routinely ask questions that I had seldom thought of asking. What will factory farming do not only to the health but the spirit of the chickens or sheep or salmon? Does the way I choose to live or work honor me? What consequences will wiping out that forest have for the lives of our seventh generation? The Traditionals' version of this principle has added some dimensions to my sense of the fitness of the things I do or say.

The way I've described the above elements of my compass may make it seem that the "cash value" it delivers is all for my world, with not much in it for me. Not so.

When I succeed in being guided by any of these principles I get the feeling of being connected to my world, a part of it, not alone. More rooted than at other times, more able to bend without breaking in a storm.

Who to talk to and how

> [In] the Ojibwa world [the] same standards which apply to mutual obligations between human beings are likewise implied in the reciprocal relations between human and other-than-human persons. [In] relations with the [powers] the individual does not expect to receive a blessing for nothing. It is not a free gift; on [your] part there are obligations to be met. There is a principle of reciprocity implied.
>
> — A. Irving Hallowell
> *Ojibwa Ontology, Behavior, and World View*[8]

What I've chosen to put in my picture of a hidden order is a simplified version of the beings that inhabit the world of the Traditionals. The entities are similar to those subscribed to by other cultures: A Great Spirit or Absolute Atman, personifications of the Sun, the Earth, and other elements of the biosphere. But what I hadn't come across elsewhere and found refreshing was how the Traditionals talked to these powers.

No kneeling or head bending or any other form of self-abasement. It pleases the Powers to see you stand tall when you address them. You speak as you would to an elder who you know cares for you. Respectfully, but without any groveling. Here's Rolling Thunder in a healing ceremony for three people, including Alice, the herbalist who often gathered medicinal plants with him.

He begins with an invocation in which he calls out to the powers of the four directions, and "To the Father Sun, To the Mother Earth." The last part of the ceremony is focused on Alice. Toward the end he looks at the sky and says in a "calm and straight and natural" way:

"We ask the Great Spirit that this woman be made free to do the work in the world that is meant for her to do ... We ask that it be that way."

The ritual goes on a bit longer. "When it was finished, Rolling Thunder said simply, 'That's all.' [Everyone] got up and walked away." [9]

Transaction over. No need at the start or at the end for any outward show of piety.

The only requirement is that the help you ask for serve some need greater than only that of your own wellbeing. You do the asking in a "sacred" manner only if the gift you seek will enable you to do something for your world.

14
Postscript

> [All] that we are and will and do depends, in the last analysis, on what we believe the Nature of Things to be.
>
> — Aldous Huxley, *The Perennial Philosophy*[1]

My picture of an unseen order is idiosyncratically mine. It feels that way though most of its elements are not my creations. But they are in the picture because they meet my inclusion criteria.

I found no objective way to settle the question of whether or not a force or principle or power that got included actually existed. I could find reasons to think it might be out there, to make the notion of its existence seem plausible. But thought could take me no further, so the decision to make it part of my operating reality had to be based on what my feelings said about it.

The composition of my unseen order is not fixed. As I learn more about the physical world, from others and from my experiences, I find reasons to tinker with its make-up. I like the idea of a picture that can evolve along with my understanding of and intuitions about the nature of things. Makes it feel like a living thing, not a mummy wrapped in the cloth of some unyielding theology, whether imported or homemade.

My conception works for me in large measure because it is, in all these ways, mine. That's why, as I've said before, I have no wish to sell you any part of it. But there is an idea related to it that I hope you will buy, if you don't already own it. The idea is this:

If you have any need to own a picture of an "unseen order," you'll be better served if you create one than if you buy any of those offered by others. By all means make use of some of the ideas in them that appeal to you, but as elements of a collage that's uniquely yours. And establish a direct link to whatever powers you decide are out there; don't go through intermediaries.

The Indian philosopher Krishnamurti liked to point out that in many ways most of us live "secondhand" lives. We let ourselves be guided by ideas and assumptions about the way things are that we take in unwittingly or uncritically. We don't check to see if they jibe with our own experiences, intuitions, and common sense.

It's OK to let others' ideas about something become your provisional understanding of it if there are hard facts related to it about which they know more than you. Oh, is that how super-fluids behave? You won a Nobel for your studies of them? Right, I'll take on your picture of that bit of reality, at least until you or one of your peers changes it.

But when the task is to create an unseen order that will sustain your spirit, the final facts are your feelings and intuitions about the matter. This makes it a situation in which you both have an opportunity to be a "firsthand" person, and have a lot to gain by exercising that option — a belief system tailor-made for your psyche. How to increase the odds that your intuitions won't lead you astray?

I believe we all have the ability to grasp some aspects of reality directly, without the help of any instruments or teachers. The problem of course is that the screen on which our intuitions display their perceptions is the same as the one on which we project our hopes, wishes, fears, and biases. Hence the old exhortation to "know thyself." The more self-aware we are, the more likely that our intuitions reflect what's "out there" than that which is "in here."

The big obstacle in the path to self-knowledge is the fear that what you find inside will prove that you are a bad person. The fear is intensified by the tendency to equate being good with being all good, all the time. It has helped me to keep in mind that we all start out with a mix of good and bad habits, thoughts, and impulses, and that weeding out the latter is a lifelong task. And it helps to remember that the fear of finding out that you are "bad" can only arise in someone who wishes to be and therefore is essentially "good."

END

Acknowledgments

Writing this book proved to be a long slog, and I needed help along the way. It was provided by those who took the time to read and give me comments about drafts of the book at various stages of its development. They helped me to see what I was trying to say, and to whom. Hearing that there were things in the drafts that they liked provided much needed shots of encouragement. Writing can be a lonely business and there are times when you wonder whether what you have to say has relevance "out there." Reassurance about this from my readers kept me going.

Before I name them I'd like to give special thanks to one who gave me all these things plus the gift of the space I needed for the project: my wife, Elizabeth Eisler.

The others in my family of readers:

Laura Augustine, Michael Chambers, Joyce Cole, Erica Flock, Terri Hill, Jim Lance, Coco and Kyra Montagu, Beth Parsons, Roland Pease, Jonathan Schwartz, and Sally Walker.

I would also like to thank Nina Jaffe, who brought to the proofreading not only her keen eye for detail but also her willingness to go beyond that jurisdiction in many helpful ways.

References

Introduction

1. Nancy Harbert, In Despair Over the Polar Bear, *Time* Science & Space, August 17, 2007. (http://www.time.com/time/health/article/0,8599,1654087,00.html)

Chapter 1: **Was the problem what it seemed to be?**

1.The two books were:
George M. Prince, *The Practice of Creativity* (New York: Harper & Row, 1970)
William J. J. Gordon, *Synectics: The Development of Creative Potential* (New York: Harper & Brothers, 1961).

2C.J. Jung, *Modern Man in Search of a Soul* (New York: Harcourt, Brace & World, 1933).

3.Gail Sheehy, *Passages: Predictable Crises of Adult Life* (New York: E.P. Dutton, 1976).

Chapter 2: **What I learned in the querencia**

1.Abraham H. Maslow:
a) *Motivation and Personality*, Second Edition (New York: Harper & Row, 1970).
b) *Toward a Psychology of Being* (New York: Van Nostrand, 1962).
c) *The Farther Reaches of Human Nature* (New York, Penguin, 1976).

2.Viktor Frankl, *Man's Search for Meaning* (New York: Simon and Schuster, 1962).

3.____________, *The Will to Meaning* (New York: New American Library, 1970).

4. ____________, *The Unheard Cry for Meaning* (New York: Simon and Schuster, 1978).

5.Timothy Lent, ed., *Viktor E. Frankl Anthology* (Bloomington, IN: Xlibris 2004).

6.John (Fire) Lame Deer and Richard Erdoes, *Lame Deer: Seeker of Visions* (New York: Simon and Schuster, 1972).

Chapter 3: **Ways out of the impasse**

1.William James, *Essays on Faith and Morals*, Selected by R.B. Perry (New York: New American Library, Meridian Printing, 1962).

2. William James, *The Varieties of Religious Experience: A Study in Human Nature*, Gifford Lectures, Edinburgh, 1901–1902 (New York: Random House, Paperback Edition, 2002).

Chapter 4: **The end of a phase**

1.A.J. Chopra, *Managing the People Side of Innovation: 8 Rules for Engaging Minds and Hearts*,(West Hartford, CT: Kumarian Press, 1999).

Chapter 5: Creating a live hypothesis

1. David Bohm and B.J. Hiley, *The Undivided Universe: An Ontological Interpretation of Quantum Theory* (Abingdon and New York: Routledge, 1993).
2. William James, op. cit. (*Essays*).
3. Fritjof Capra, *The Tao of Physics* (Boulder, CO: Shambhala, Bantam Edition, 1977).
4. Ken Wilber, ed., *The Holographic Paradigm and other paradoxes* (Boulder, CO: Shambhala, 1982).
5. Ken Wilber, ed., *Quantum Questions: Mystical Writings of the World's Great Physicists* (Boulder, CO: Shambhala, 1984).
6. Sir Arthur Eddington, *New Pathways in Science* (Cambridge: Cambridge University Press, 1935).
7. James Jeans in Albert Einstein et al., *Living Philosophies* (New York: Simon and Schuster, 1931).
8. James Jeans, *The Mysterious Universe* (Cambridge: Cambridge University Press, 1939).
9. Sir Arthur Eddington, *Science and the Unseen World* (New York: Macmillan, 1929).
10. Erwin Schroedinger, *Mind and Matter* (Cambridge: Cambridge University Press, 1958).
11. James Jeans, op. cit. (*Mysterious Universe*).
12. Sir Arthur Eddington op. cit. (*New Pathways*).

13. A.E. Eddington, *The Nature of the Physical World* (New York: Macmillan, 1929).

Chapter 6: **Things to keep in mind**

1. William James, op. cit. (*Essays*)

Chapter 7: **Selecting your sources**

1. Barre Toelken in *Seeing with a Native Eye* — Essays on Native Religion, W.H. Capps, ed. (New York: Harper & Row, 1976).
2. Ruth Beebe Hill, *Hanta Yo: An American Saga* (Garden City, New York: Doubleday, 1979).
3. There are the classics: *Book of the Hopi* by Frank Waters (1963), and *Black Elk Speaks* by John G. Neihardt (1932). Both books made me rethink my ideas about the nature of things, but their impact was more intellectual than visceral. Some of those that drew me more fully into the traditional world and that are not cited elsewhere in this book include:

   The Desert Smells Like Rain, by Gary Paul Nabham (Berkeley: North Point Press, 1982).

   A Pima Remembers, by George Webb (Tucson: University of Arizona Press, 1982).

   The Other Side of Eden, by Hugh Brody (New York: Farrar, Strauss and Giroux, 2000)

   People of the Deer, by Farley Mowat (New York, Jove Publications, 1978).

   Singing for Power, by Ruth Murray Underhill (Berkeley: University of California Press, paperback edition, 1976).
4. Charles C. Mann, 1491: *New Revelations of the Americas Before Columbus* (New York: Vintage Books, 2006). See Chapter 1: A View from Above, pp. 3–22, and Chapter 9: Amazonia, pp. 315–349.

Chapter 8: **A sequence of events**

1. David Bohm, *Wholeness and the Implicate Order* (London and New York: Routledge, 1980).
2. Joseph Epes Brown, in *I Become Part of It*, D.M. Dooling and P.

Jordan-Smith eds. (New York: Parabola Books, 1989).

3. Gerald Feinberg and Robert Shapiro, *Life Beyond Earth: The Intelligent Earthling's Guide to Life in the Universe* (New York: William Morrow, 1980).
4. Ruth Beebe Hill, op. cit. (*Hanta Yo*).
5. Lewis Thomas, *The Lives of a Cell: Notes of a Biology Watcher* (Toronto/New York/London: Bantam Books, 1975).

Chapter 9: **The premise**

1. Barre Toelken, op. cit. (*Seeing With a Native Eye*).
2. Barry Lopez, Story at Anaktuvuk Pass, in *The Graywolf Annual Three: Essays, Memoirs & Reflections*, Scott Walker, ed. (Saint Paul, MN: Graywolf Press, 1986).

Chapter 10: **Pruning the interior landscape**

1. H.G. Wells, *The Outline of History* (New York: Macmillan, 1921).
2. Donald G. Kaufman and Cecilia M. Franz, *The Biosphere: Protecting Our Global Environment*, Fourth Edition (Dubuque, IA: Kendall/Hunt, 2005).
3. Joseph Bruchac, in *I Become Part of It*, op. cit.
4. Ashley Montagu, Darwin: *Competition and Cooperation* (Westport, CT: Greenwood Press, 1975).
5. Elizabeth Marshall Thomas, *The Harmless People*, Revised Edition (New York: Vintage Books, 1989).
6. Doug Boyd, *Rolling Thunder* (New York: Dell, 1974).
7. The WILD Foundation (www.wild.org/main/how-wild-works/policy-research/wilderness-and-climate-change/).
8. Harvey Locke and Brendan Mackey, The Nature of Climate Change, *International Journal of Wilderness*, Vol. 15, No. 2, August 2009, pp. 7–13/40.
9. Richard P. Novitzki, R. Daniel Smith, and Judy D. Fretwell, Restoration, Creation, and Recovery of Wetlands: Wetland Functions, Values, and Assessment, *U.S. Geological Survey Water Supply Paper 2425*, 1997 (water.usgs.gov/nwsum/WSP2425/functions.html).

10. John Carter, *Nature Trails*, Eugene Natural History Society, Vol. 45, No. 8, November 2010.

11. Barry Holstun Lopez, Of Wolves and Men (New York: Charles Scribner's Sons, 1978).

12. L. David Mech, *The Wolf: The Ecology and Behavior of an Endangered Species* (Minneapolis: University of Minnesota Press edition, 1981).

13. Robert L. Beschta, William J. Ripple, Large predators and trophic cascades in terrestrial ecosystems of the Western United States, *Biological Conservation*, 142 (12), November 2009, pp. 2401–2414.

14. John Carter, op. cit.

15. Farley Mowat, *Never Cry Wolf* (New York, Bantam Books, 1979).

Chapter 11: **Speeding the shift**

1. Paul J. Crutzen and Christian Schwägerl, Living in the Anthropocene: Toward a New Global Ethos, *Yale Environment 360*, January 24, 2011. (e360.yale.edu/feature/living_in_the_anthropocene_toward_a_new_global_ethos/2363/).

2. Joseph F.C. Dimento and Pamela Doughman, *Making Climate Change Understandable, in Climate Change: What It Means for Us, Our Children, and Our Grandchildren*, Dimento and Doughman, eds. (Cambridge, MA: MIT Press, 2007), pp. 1–9.

3. James Lovelock, *The Vanishing Face of Gaia: A Final Warning* (New York: Basic Books, 2009).

4. Duane Elgin: *Voluntary Simplicity: Toward a Way of Life that is Outwardly Simple, Inwardly Rich* (New York: William Morrow, 1981).

5. Amitai Etzioni, A New Social Movement?, in *The Poetic Alternative to Consumer Culture*, Samuel Alexander ed. (Whanganui, NZ: Stead and Daughters, 2009), pp. 619–643.

6. Paul R. Abramson and Ronald Inglehart, *Value Change in Global Perspective* (Ann Arbor, MI: University of Michigan Press, 1995).

7. Amitai Etzioni, *A Crisis of Consumerism, in Aftershocks: Economic Crisis and Institutional Choice*, Anton Hemerijk, Ben Knapen, and Ellen van Doon, eds. (Amsterdam: Amsterdam University Press, 2010), pp. 155–162.

8. Sheldon Kamieniecki and Michael Kraft, Foreword, in *Climate Change*, op. cit.

9. Johan Rockström et al. A safe operating space for humanity, in *Nature*, Vol. 461, September 24, 2009, pp. 472–475.

10. Elizabeth Kolbert, *Field Notes from a Catastrophe: Man, Nature, and Climate Change* (New York and London: Bloomsbury, 2006).

11. Pew Research Center Polls:

October 2010 (www.people-press.org/2010/10/27/little-change-in-opinions-about-global-warming).

October 2012 (www.people-press.org/2012/10/15/more-say-there-is-solid-evidence-of-global-warming).

12. Gallup Environment Polls, 2001–2012 summary: (http://www.gallup.com/poll/1615/environment.aspx).

13. Peter T. Doran and Maggie Kendall Zimmerman, Examining the Scientific Consensus on Climate Change, Transactions American Geophysical Union, *Eos*,Vol. 90, No.3. January 20, 2009, pp. 22–23.

14. Robin Lloyd, Why Are Americans So Ill-Informed about Climate Change? *Scientific American*, February 23, 2011. (www.scientificamerican.com/article.cfm?id=why-are-americans-so-ill).

15. Andrew C. Revkin, Climate Change as News: Challenges in Communicating Environmental Science, in *Climate Change*, op. cit. (pp. 139–159).

16. Doug Boyd, op. cit. (*Rolling Thunder*).

17. Lewis Thomas, op. cit. (*Lives of a Cell*).

18. Kaufman and Franz, op. cit. (*The Biosphere*).

19. Ibid.

20. Population quotes from *Vermonters for a Sustainable Population* (www.vspop.org/htm/populationquotes.htm)

Chapter 12: **Reasons for hope**

1. David Bohm, *Thought as a System* (Abingdon, U.K. and New York: Routledge, 1994).
2. Oren Lyons, *Our Mother Earth, in I Become Part of It*, op. cit. (pp. 270–274).
3. Jorge Moll et al., Human fronto-mesolimbic networks guide decisions about charitable donation, *Proceedings of the National Academy of Sciences (U.S.A.)*, October 17, 2006, Vol. 103, No. 42, pp. 15623–15628.
4. J. Moll et al., *Neural Basis of Human Altruism* (https://sites.google.com/a/neuroscience-rio.org/www/research22)
5. Shankar Vedantam, If It Feels Good to Be Good, It Might Be Only Natural, *The Washington Post*, May 28, 2007 (www.washingtonpost.com/wpdyn/content/article/2007/05/27/AR20007052701056.html).
6. Harold F. Searles, *The Nonhuman Environment: In Normal Development and Schizophrenia* (Madison, CT: International Universities Press, 1960).

Chapter 13: **What I choose to believe**

1. Gerald Feinberg and Robert Shapiro, op. cit. (*Life Beyond Earth*).
2. Kaufman and Franz, op. cit. (*The Biosphere*).
3. Kate Melville, How Animals Regulate Their Own Numbers, headlines of a study of arctic ground squirrels by Tim Karels and Rudy Boonstra, in *Science a GoGo*, November 23, 2000 (www.scienceagogo.com/news/20001023043308data_trunc_sys.shtml).
4. Tim J. Karels & Rudy Boonstra, Concurrent density dependence and independence in populations of arctic ground squirrels. *Nature*, Vol. 408, 23 November, 2000, pp. 460–463.
5. Stephen J. Gould, *Ever Since Darwin: Reflections in Natural History* (New York: W.W. Norton, 1979).
6. David Bohm and B.J. Hiley, op. cit. (*The Undivided Universe*).
7. David Bohm, A New Theory of the Relationship of Mind and Matter, *Philosophical Psychology*, Vol 3, No. 2, 1990, pp. 271–286.

8. A. Irving Hallowell, Ojibwa Ontology, Behavior, and World View, in *Teachings from the American Earth*, Dennis Tedlock and Barbara Tedlock, eds. (New York: Liveright, 1975), pp. 141–178.
9. Doug Boyd, op. cit. (*Rolling Thunder*).

Chapter 14: **Postscript**

1. Aldous Huxley, *The Perennial Philosophy* (Cleveland: World Publishing, Meridian edition, 1962).

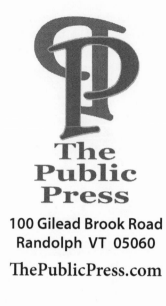

The Public Press

100 Gilead Brook Road
Randolph VT 05060

ThePublicPress.com

Promoting Free Speech Word-by-Word

We, the editors at The Public Press, are concerned that conventional book publishing has gone the way of "info-tainment." We offer a high-tech, low-impact publishing strategy as an alternative. We embrace new technologies and the economies of scale – "small" scale, that is – to publish books that might not otherwise see the light of day. Our titles are then made available to the public via traditional book trade channels.

About the Public Press

Our founding fathers had the infinite wisdom to make freedom of speech one of our inalienable rights. To a great extent we have unwittingly sold that right to commercial interests that replace free speech with a "free" message that promotes their proprietary financial interests. Slowly, but surely, we are losing not only our free speech, but all other freedoms as well.

Our Purpose

Empower authors

The Public Press puts the fewest possible filters or impediments between the creator and audience. The Public does not control the publishing process in the same way that a commercial publisher does. As a result there are stylistic and quality variations from title to title. The resulting books are like hearth-baked bread or handcrafted beer compared to more uniform, but less distinctive, products of commercial counterparts.

Treat authors as partners

The Public Press is destined to become an author co-operative, where the authors are business partners with the publisher, not licensees paid a small percentage royalty on the sales of books. The Public Press offers an alternative to the traditional author/publisher model.

Leave the lightest possible footprint

Book publishing, historically, has been a notoriously inefficient industry from the standpoint of resource consumption. A book can travel across the country only to be returned, unsold, to its original point of shipment. The Public Press strives for economies of scale-small scale. New technologies have made available writing and editing tools, print on demand options, improved communications, and new sales outlets that make it possible for publishing to be a model of resource efficiency.

Shout from the highest tree

The Public Press is comprised of a community of individuals who share certain values (such as an appreciation for independent thought and freedom of speech) but who may not share geography or demography. The success of The Public Press is entirely dependent on our ability to reach these people and to convince them to involve others. As opposed to our namesake counterparts, National Public Radio and Public Television, The Public Press receives no government funding.

Frequently Asked Questions

What is The Public Press?

The Public Press is a printed word counterpart to Public Television or Public Radio, but operating strictly on a pay-as-you-go, grassroots basis. It empowers authors whose work is deserving of publication but is not, by the standards of traditional publishing, commercially viable.

What is wrong with traditional publishing?

Nothing is "wrong," but the publishing business has gotten too big, too consolidated, and too enslaved to an economic system that caters to the mass market. While the industry serves the broad midsection of the market very well, it no longer accommodates the public interests that exist on the fringe.

Don't small presses fill the uncovered niches?

Some do, and very well. Bold and adventurous small presses fill specific editorial niches, and our hats are off to them! Because they are subject to industry-wide trading terms that favor the large houses, only the most efficient, well-managed, and highly focused small presses thrive. There are many large information gaps left in between the good small presses. These are the gaps that The Public Press will fill.

Are small presses capable of having hit books?

Absolutely, but even when successful, the window of opportunity will be small before the mainstream publishers jump on the bandwagon. Feng shui and aromatherapy were new ideas introduced by small, innovative publishers. Once the market was demonstrated, commercial presses quickly followed suit. Now, just a few years later, a search on Amazon shows nearly 4000 available titles for each subject!

Are too many books published?

More than 250,000 new titles are published every year! Despite this onslaught of new titles, the range of information covered is narrowing. The majority of these titles lose money for their publishers and receive only a brief period of exposure in the marketplace. Authors, who put all their investment of time and energy at the front end of the process, become frustrated, because their books never find their natural audiences.

Why do publishers publish books that lose money?

The traditional publishing world is divided into blockbusters and longshots. 5% of the titles (the blockbusters) account for 95% of the sales. 95% (the longshots) scramble for what is left.

Occasionally a title breaks from the pack and becomes a blockbuster. For every Harry Potter, there are thousands of books that slip beneath the waves and are quickly relegated to the remainder shelves.

How does a book become a huge hit?

The most reliable path to success is to piggyback on free publicity generated by presence in the mass media. Recently the *New York Times* Best-Seller list had three books "written" by professional wrestlers! Their sales success is directly tied to their television exposure.

So celebrity = success?

Sports heroes, film stars, and high-profile politicians have no trouble getting book deals for their exercise plans, special diets, theories of religion, or juicy memoirs. Also, there are superstar writers (Stephen King, John Grisham, Patricia Cornwell) who have developed their own brands and franchises.

So how will The Public Press succeed?

There is no shortage of interesting people doing worthwhile things. Most of these people, even those who write their stories very well, are shut out of the commercial publishing business. These are the people who will become our "celebrities," meaning that we will celebrate what they have accomplished.

The Public Press will give these authors (and their potential readerships) a new option, a home, promotion, and a context.

Will The Public Press add to the noise and clutter of the world?

No, The Public Press will add to the richness of the cultural fabric by making it easier for an author to publish a book or to bring an out-of-print title back. It will do so in a way that leaves the lightest possible footprint. No book will be printed before it is sold. There will be no warehouses of books to be remaindered. The notoriously wasteful "gone today, here tomorrow" cycle of the book business will be avoided entirely.

Who started The Public Press?

Stephen Morris is the founder of The Public Press. You can learn more about him at ThePublicPress.com.

About the Author

A.J. ("Jeet") Chopra is a Cambridge-based consultant whose specialty is identifying the thought process used by successful inventors. He describes himself as an innovation catalyst.

He is a former partner in the company Synectics, Inc., a word defined in the *Random House Dictionary* as "the study of creative processes, especially as applied to the solution of problems by a group of diverse individuals." His ideas and management practices are featured in his book, *Managing the People Side of Innovation* (Kumarian Press, 1999).

However, as he was helping others find solutions to their problems, he was developing one of his own, an overwhelming despondency about the enormous environmental challenges facing our planet, a syndrome that has given rise to the term "eco-despair." *Moving to the Earth's Beat* is Chopra's journey to the brink of this emotional precipice, and how he found a path back to safety and sanity by re-examining the problem from a diverse set of viewpoints, including those of psychologists, physicists, and traditional Native Americans.

The story is uniquely Chopra's, but the solutions he uncovers will be helpful for anyone who feels that Earth is imperiled by the toxic and wasteful practices of *Homo Sap*.